Bad-mouthing: The Language
of Special Needs

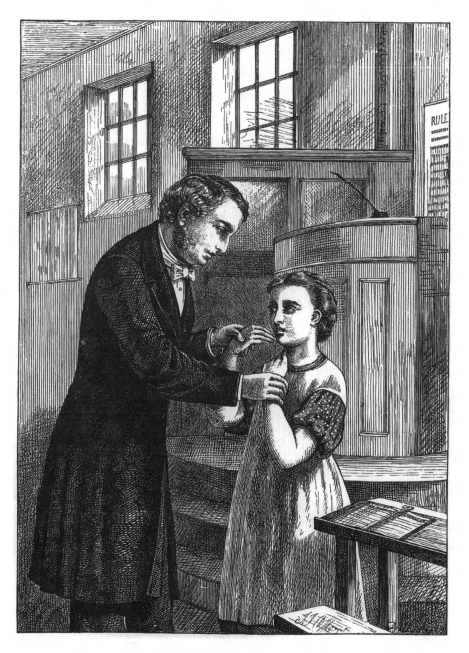

TEACHING THE DUMB TO SPEAK

To Sue,
with love

Bad-mouthing:
The Language of Special Needs

Jenny Corbett

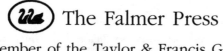 The Falmer Press

(A member of the Taylor & Francis Group)

London • Washington, D.C.

USA   The Falmer Press, 4 John St, London WC1N 2ET

UK   The Falmer Press, Taylor & Francis Inc., 1900 Frost Road, Suite 101, Bristol, PA 19007

© J. Corbett 1996

First published 1996

A catalogue record of this publication is available from the British Library

ISBN 0 7507 0501 9 cased
ISBN 0 7507 0502 7 paper

Library of Congress Cataloging-in-Publication Data are available on request

Jacket design by Caroline Archer

The cover artwork first appeared in Bartley, G. (1871) *The Schools for the People*, London, Bell & Daldy, p. 399.

Typeset in 11/13 pt Garamond by Graphicraft Typesetters Ltd., Hong Kong

Printed in Great Britain by Biddles Ltd., Guildford and King's Lynn on paper which has a specified pH value on final paper manufacture of not less than 7.5 and is therefore 'acid-free'.

Contents

Acknowledgments

The author and publishers would like to thank the following for permission to reproduce their material:

The Editors of the *Oxford Review of Education* for 'Equality Fifteen Years On', from the *ORE*, 17 (2).
Alison Silverwood for 'Searching for Disability Arts'.
Alyson Publications, Inc. for 'This Strong Beam of Light' by Raymond Luczak from *Eyes of Desire: A Deaf Gay and Lesbian Reader*.
Random House, Inc. for 'No Pity' by Joseph P. Shapiro.
Micheline Mason for 'What's it got to do with you dear?'.
Willard J. Madsen for 'You Have to be Deaf to Understand'.
Deborah Levin for John Callaghan's 'Cowboys and Wheelchair' cartoon.

Preface

Delicate words exhausted through over-use.
Bawdy words made temperate by repetition.
Enchanting and enchanted words wand broken.
Words of the spirit forced into the flesh.
Words of the flesh unlovely in a white gown.
Slang in a sling shot hurled and hurled and hurled.
That is the legacy of the dead.

Jeanette Winterson
1994, Art and Lies, p. 65

Foreword

This book is about language and, in turn, the manipulation, the power strategies, the cruelty, the defensiveness, the blind alleys down which we are in danger of sending ourselves as we grapple with relentless changes. It is called *Bad-mouthing* the means by which the dominant discourse is maintained by the established elite no matter the current fashion whether it be eighteenth century paternalism or late twentieth century political correctness. One of the principal methods of Bad-mouthing is by labelling people, bracketing them into defined sectors to enhance our significance.

This is not a comforting book to read tucked up in bed with a glass of malt whisky or a cup of camomile tea. This is a disturbing book, an honest book, a book that will alter perceptions and practice. Writing in a refreshingly direct language and style, Jenny Corbett challenges our interpretation of the word 'special' and demands that we recognize that sentimentality, arrogance and fear are rooted in society's suppression of disabled people. We are urged to compare Warnock with the new voices of disabled theorists; to appreciate the conflict between the medical model and disability culture; to listen, see, touch, feel and harken to the metaphors now being used by disabled people as we take command of our lives.

During the twentieth century we have witnessed the successive liberation paths of women, black peoples, and gays and lesbians. Disabled people have been left behind, and amongst disabled people mental health system survivors and people with special needs (who embrace all cultures, classes, races and disabilities) are the most oppressed — often denied the most basic civil rights. Disabled activists and artists, often the same individuals, are articulating powerful messages: demanding access in the very widest sense, civil liberties, and the right to control their own lives.

In a culture where powerful vested interests have forged careers, wealth and reputations 'caring' for disabled people, this activism is a threat to entrenched influence and paternalism. The great and the good, the medical professionals, the media personalities, and the do-gooders will not easily relinquish their power base. They will go to great lengths using combinations of sophistry and crudity in attempts to subvert the inevitable transfer of power.

Language is power, Jenny Corbett reminds us. Utilizing a well chosen eclectic series of example texts, we are introduced to a variety of voices from the disabled community. The questions she poses on these texts are judiciously selected, and both teacher and student will enjoy grappling with exciting new ways of looking at language and as a consequence new ways of looking at life.

Poetry and music are particularly effective means of enabling new voices to emerge from centuries of oppression. There are several poems quoted in *Bad-mouthing*. I particularly liked those by Char March, Willard J Masden, and Paulette Ng, which are effective in evoking the spiritual power of language now used in education, advocacy and political campaigning.

Johnny Crescendo, a celebrated activist, singer and poet, writes and sings about the **white coats** who prescribe and monitor, about the **charity personalities** and how we must **piss on pity**, and ironically tells the world why **disabled people aren't allowed to say fuck**. Thousands of disabled people, in Britain and abroad, are inspired by his words; by the language that is changing their lives now.

Society labels me **Writer, Poet, Director, Adviser**; accurate descriptions, conferring status and respect, acceptable to the worlds of literature and charities. My own labels are Survivor and Crip; terms used by fellow disabled people and mental health system survivors.

I am privileged to be asked to write this Foreword and this has arisen, I venture to guess, from my willingness to accept both sets of labels. It wasn't always so. Fifteen years ago I was labelled **Engineer** and **Commercial Director**, a corporation man concealing years of psychiatric experiences and unaware of the physical disability yet to come. I have made major changes. I have learnt to welcome changes, changes that are grist to the mill of the soul. I welcome this book which will be of value to the academic, the student, the teacher, the legislator and, not least, to the general public.

A decade ago I published a poem entitled *Label Me*. Jenny Corbett has asked me to quote an extract which has particular resonances:

> . . . .
> I know I'm a hype target
> realise I'm the clone
> they need to feed
> their insidious imagery

I won't be conned again
I'll never wear those faceless clothes.
Don't expect me to reveal
My own sensitive personality

I got this friend called Frank
who prints paper and assorted graffiti.
He made me a lovely T-shirt
It said . . .
    I'm a drone — use me, screw me.

Bad-mouthing is an important contribution. It has already changed my perception.

Joe Bidder
© *1995*

Introduction: Bad-mouthing

I have called this book 'Bad-mouthing' because it is about the use of language in relation to concepts of disability. We are in a period of history where, with increased political awareness in the use of language, we try now to reconstruct the terms we use and the imagery that is created.

The image on the cover has been selected specifically to convey the challenges we now face. It was used in an educational text of 1871 and was an illustration of what were then perceived as innovative practices. For us now, viewing the image with an awareness of the influence of disability politics, the picture demonstrates paternalism and oppression.

Its caption, 'Teaching the Dumb to Speak', is ripe for the most rigorous deconstruction. Special educational practice from the late 1800s to the present may be said to embody this sentiment. From a punitive emphasis upon oralism in the teaching of deaf students, to a meticulous approach to individual learning programmes, to a focus on advocacy and empowerment, special education can be seen over the last hundred years or so to have been concerned with 'teaching the dumb to speak' at both a literal and metaphorical level. That this is now couched in the language of 'empowerment' does not, for me anyway, negate its inherent paternalism and potential to oppress.

My particular interest in the language of special needs has developed over the last few years, during which time I have explored the ways in which new discourses have emerged to challenge those of enlightened modernity (Corbett, 1993); the political correctness of special language in the mid-1990s (Corbett, 1994a); and, the ways in which imagery is changing as proud labels displace the legacy of negativity (Corbett, 1994b). These are all complex issues, which need to be contextualized both politically and historically, requiring a level of analysis which moves beyond an investigation of surface semantics. In this book I shall develop the ideas I introduced in these initial explorations to build an analysis of where the language of special needs has emerged from, where it seems to be going at present and what is likely to become of it in the near future.

Looking at Language

The way in which words are used to define, portray and explain people and situations is an endless source of fascination to me. The power of language is overwhelming. It is used by politicians and the media to create emotional responses. None of us are immune to the force of verbal imagery.

'Special Needs' is a term which has become a short-hand for 'Special Educational Needs', as defined within the Warnock Report (DES, 1978). The inclusion of the word 'educational' tends to be used as a justification for distinguishing some 'needs' as 'special'. It is argued that the 'specialness' is purely educational and not generalized into the broader community.

Whilst there has been considerable theorizing on the psychological and sociological aspects of special education (e.g., Mittler, 1974; Tomlinson, 1982) as well as a recognition of the influence of policies (Fulcher, 1989) and politics (Barton, 1988), there has not yet been a concerted attempt to analyse the way in which language is used to create images and codes. In his cumulative examinations of conceptualizing 'integration', Booth (e.g., 1981, 1987, 1988, 1992) has prepared the way for such an analysis to develop. This general lack of interest may be because semantics seem peripheral to special education: the focus has been rather on individual case studies, teaching programmes, legislation and practice. Indeed, as the changes brought about by the 1988 Education Act influence special education, there has been an increasing tendency to examine curricular issues, assessment methods and the fine details of responding to equality initiatives (e.g., Ainscow and Florek, 1989; Wolfendale, 1993; Claire, Maybin and Swann, 1993).

Why, then, should I wish to explore the language of special needs when it may appear to others to be a marginal issue? I feel that the language we use expresses our confidence, caution, commitment or doubt. It says what we feel now, even where it is a dissembling language. The very directness of it expresses tangible unease for many educators. 'Special needs' is becoming a most unacceptable term. Most prefer the words 'learning support'. However, these words apply specifically to the *provision*, not to the *people*. Teachers are unlikely to say, 'He has learning support', but use the term 'special needs' or 'learning difficulties'.

There is a genuine anxiety about the level of government and institutional commitment to 'special needs' where cuts have to be made and educational establishments are being measured on performance. Integration has been spoken of as a national goal since the 1981

Education Act, yet it remains patchy, insecure and emerges unsupported by policy frameworks. What seems to have happened to 'special needs' is that it tends to be viewed as a marginal issue, which is expendable in a crisis.

In order to more fully understand why some learners are marginalized and given an inferior status, it is important to explore the way in which language has been used. The language of 'special needs' has to be rigorously deconstructed to reveal the uncomfortable emotions within its imagery. What does 'special' mean? If we detach this word from its anchor in 'educational' we can see that 'special' does not mean especially good and valued unless we use a phrase like, 'you are a special person'. It is linked to 'needs' which implies dependency, inadequacy and unworthiness.

I think we have to recognize the duel elements of 'special needs' and the dangers that lie within both. Firstly, there is the sentimental language of 'special need' which is embodied in the imagery of protection, care, tenderness and love. I dislike and suspect sentimentality. I think it is a sham emotion and one which tends to mask cold, callous indifference. This language needs to be examined and revealed for the sugar-coated poison that it is. Secondly, and this is the mirror-image of such sentiment, there is hate. The language of 'special needs' has always been composed of words and images which foster fear, mistrust, loathing and hostility. 'Idiot', 'imbecile' and 'moron' are used as terms of abuse, just as 'nigger', 'queer' and 'spastic' are. I think it is essential to disengage 'special needs' from its 'educational' base and place it in a wider social and cultural context, in order to appreciate how pervasive and damaging these dual elements are.

If 'special needs' are words which require a wider interpretation than the merely 'educational', where are the boundaries to be drawn? The focus might be on international differences in the use of language, on a historical reflection, or on the politics of language. Although I shall include elements of all these dimensions, it is my intention to focus upon the influence of new discourses, personal narratives and the use of metaphor.

Mouthing Prejudice

We need to listen to what we say. Unless we consciously hear our own words, we are unable and unwilling to question what feelings are revealed beneath ill-considered mouthing.

Just as there has been a deliberate awareness, among those who aspire to politically correct language, of any words which connect 'black' with negativity, so the way in which we refer to people as 'idiot' or 'fool' needs to be understood as a reflection of social conditioning. When we say 'You idiot!', it is usually a spontaneous comment, often used with affection. We tend not to consider from where it derived nor why we continue to use this expression.

Whilst words such as 'idiot', 'cretin', 'moron', 'fool' and 'imbecile', were once the familiar, pseudo-scientific, professional language of doctors, they now remain as part of our colloquial speech. Once terms of categorization and medical definition, they are now blatant and crude terms of abuse. We need to recognize this and reflect upon it if we are to understand why an integrated society, let alone an integrated education system, is so difficult to achieve. Our social structure, in the Western world, thrives upon hierarchies. We measure our social success in relation to others in the hierarchy. The extent to which we are richer, more clever, better housed and higher in status is an indicator of our social standing, power and value. Without a pecking order, we would not feel good about our superiority to others lower down the hierarchy.

When do we habitually use words such as, 'You idiot!' or 'moron'? Is it when we feel angry that others have misunderstood our meanings? Have they been slow to grasp ideas we are trying to express? Was their behaviour inexplicable? Did they reveal weaknesses such as absent-mindedness, forgetfulness or confusion? Were they too nakedly human?

The other day I was watching monkeys in London Zoo playing behind bars whilst humans observed their behaviour. The baby monkey was absorbed in the game of pulling the adult monkey's faeces out of its anus and eating them. A mother with her own baby in a pushchair watched with disgust and said, 'Horrible child', immediately equating the infant monkey's behaviour with that of infant humans. It is disturbing for us, as human beings, to acknowledge our own animal natures, our vulnerabilities and basic instincts.

One of the most basic of instincts is fear. It eats into us and destroys our peace of mind. It acts as a warning for us of possible danger. We react instinctively by fight or flight. Among our most deep-seated fears is that of the unfamiliar. This is why we push down into our subconscious mind all those uncomfortable feelings we are not sure how to address. It is easier to block them out and pretend they are not there. This is also why there is so much fear about people who are different. They may be different from a conventional norm in their intellectual, physical, sexual or racial characteristics. Their very difference is a provocation for it touches on those fears of that which is unfamiliar and deeply buried inside all of us. Their strangeness is our strangeness — visible rather than hidden.

It is not surprising that fear of difference breeds hostility. If we are competing in a social hierarchy which idealizes human strengths and conceptualizes an image of physical and intellectual perfection encapsulated in a stereotypical norm, then we want no reminders of human fragility or diversity, in ourselves or others. Indeed, it is useful to see some people as intrinsically inferior. This distinguishes us from them. We are one kind of human whilst they are another form altogether. If this detachment is carried further they become a form of human being no longer requiring compassion or dignity. Thus doctors were able to apply a detached judgment to the needs of 'morons' and 'idiots' if their intellectual status rendered them less than human. This level of detachment was taken to its ultimate extreme in the Nazi murders of people who were different racially, intellectually, physically and sexually. The images of human perfection being promoted by them were a demonstration of that desperate fear of the unfamiliar and adherence to a rigid concept of the desired norm.

I would not wish us all to become so anxious about our display of verbal political correctness that we never again permit ourselves to say 'You idiot!' After all, we often say it in relation to our own behaviour. It can be a way of laughing at our own human frailty. We expect ourselves to measure up well and become exasperated when we behave in ways which we feel make us look foolish. Perhaps it is important for us all to recognize that in some aspects of our lives, we are all 'idiots', 'morons', 'fools' and 'imbeciles' — in other words, we are all fragile human beings. We all make mistakes and behave in ways we later regret. When we chastise ourselves by saying, 'You idiot!' we need to be gentle to ourselves as well. If we can be sympathetic and understanding towards those elements of difference and variance from an unreal perfection inside us all, we can transfer this tolerance outside ourselves to others.

My hypothesis is that 'special needs' is the language of sentimentality and prejudice. I shall illustrate this through exploring the relationship between the dominant discourse and divergent discourses which reflect the language of oppression and a struggle for recognition. I want to demonstrate that the language of 'special needs' has to change and become subverted by those who have been oppressed by it. The dominant discourse can no longer retreat into the security of 'special *educational* needs', for education is inextricably linked to the wider community, to popular culture and the politics of difference.

Speaking to an Audience

My reasons for writing this book do not stem solely from a long-term interest in the use of language. They also involve my teaching and learning experience at the University of East London. In the last four years I have been teaching units on 'Special Needs in Education' alongside a new unit that I have developed with disabled colleagues, called 'Disability Culture'. From teaching these two units week by week, I have become increasingly interested in the complex relationship between the dominant discourse of special education and the dissenting discourses of disability politics.

In writing this book, I hope to challenge the students I teach and those in other institutions to examine and reflect upon the language they habitually use. I want them to make connections between the specifically 'educational' language of 'special needs', with its known perimeters, and the political and cultural discourses of disability activists opening up concepts of community and communication. If educators saw themselves as 'teaching the dumb to speak', do disabled activists see themselves as 'teaching the arrogant to listen'?

In this book, I want readers to closely examine the way in which words are used. I shall try not to get choked up with jargon as I do not feel that is helpful — I want to communicate as clearly as possible. As a stimulus to students and as an illustration of the use of special needs language each chapter will conclude with a brief example of the language that has been the focus for discussion and a series of questions which could be addressed in relation to it.

1   The Voice of Enlightened Modernity

Introduction

In this chapter, I shall begin by suggesting why I feel that an analysis of language itself, as a means of power and definition, is of value in an evaluation of 'special needs' in the mid-1990s. In order to contextualize this discussion, examples of the relationship between the language of patronage and provision for those with 'special needs' will be examined. I shall then present what I term 'The Warnock model', being an assessment of the impact that Warnock has made on 'special needs' language and concepts over the last twenty years. Warnock represents for 'special needs' in the late twentieth century, the voice of enlightened modernity. As such, this voice dominates the special needs' discourse and needs to be challenged by competing voices in new and diverse discourses on special language.

Is there a distinct language of 'special needs' with a vocabulary and imagery of its own? To argue that there is may seem to be stretching credulity to its limit. Yet I suggest that it is the social construction and conceptualization accorded to 'special needs' that demonstrates the extent to which a language had been developed to sustain, contain and control it.

When the Warnock Report (DES, 1978) declared that the term 'special educational needs' would replace out-dated language such as 'handicapped' and 'educationally subnormal' it was heralded as a progressive move towards a more inclusive and supportive approach. The argument was that placing an emphasis upon 'educational' would indicate that it was only in relation to teaching and learning that 'special needs' were perceived. The emphasis was upon the educational experience in isolation from other contextual factors of race, class, gender and sexuality. The language of 'special educational needs' may be placed alongside the language of 'assimilation'. It is, simultaneously, about making the same but making a model of difference.

I shall be arguing, through an analysis of emerging discourses, that the emphasis upon 'special *educational* needs' was to make a lasting

7

imprint upon attitudes to disability. It is the language of the status quo — the voice of a confident and complacent establishment. The inference in the language of 'special educational needs' is that there is a consensus about 'educational needs' in the first place. It is the rhetoric of 'equal opportunity', with an underlying assumption about what all should aspire to achieve. As such, it offers a two-edged sword: it has served to cut away the sentimental divisiveness of old attitudes to 'handicap'; and, in turn, it has fostered a Eurocentric, narrowly value-laden and, sometimes, oppressive special curriculum.

I think it is useful, especially at this turbulent stage of educational history, to reassess what special language has done for and to practice. I emphasize '*practice*' for it would be only too easy to become preoccupied with a purely theoretical debate and lose contact with practical and pragmatic issues altogether. By offering examples of how the special language influenced practice, I want to reflect back on the last twenty years and see where certain images led practitioners, both for good and for ill. If we can see both the benefits and the weaknesses of the special language of the past, we are placed in a better position to select whatever was useful and discard a vocabulary which holds us back.

A Special Teacher in the Late 1970s

It is my intention to include personal narrative within this book for this seems to me to be a most appropriate way to explore and analyse the use of language by including stories and life history. Sometimes these will be stories that others have told me about their experiences. In describing the history of special language, I shall also draw upon stories of my own life history, professional encounters and conceptualization of 'special' vocabulary.

What was I doing as a teacher in a special school at the time when the Warnock Report was published? Between 1977 and 1982 I was teaching in a school for pupils with 'severe learning difficulties'. I was placed in charge of what was called the 'special care' department. This consisted of four classes, two for children with multiple disabilities, many of them in wheelchairs and two for younger and older children with disruptive behaviours. It was customary for teachers in the school to select the most awkward and time-consuming pupils to come into the 'special care' department. When I came to the school in 1977, the vocabulary being used in relation to this group was about 'care', 'nursing', 'comfort', 'respite for parents', 'occupy' and 'control'. This was the official language. The unofficial was expressed in terms such as 'dumping ground', 'sin-bin', 'vegetables', 'shitty work' and 'baby-minding'. The term 'ineducable' had been in use, specifically by the medical profession, up until the 1971 Act, which deemed all children to be able to benefit from education in some form of schooling. The pupils in my 'special care' department were those who, only a few years before, would have been cared for at home or in hospital and labelled as 'ineducable'.

How did the language of 'special educational needs' influence this group? I feel that it had a profound and quite dramatic impact. Around the time of the publication of the Warnock Report, a number of new approaches and research projects were developing which were to significantly change attitudes and practice. Getting rid of the old categories and rejecting 'ineducable' as a concept led to imaginative and innovative ways of using vocabulary: the 'special' language was the language of success, achievement and, above all, 'mastery of skills'! Perhaps two of the most useful examples of this new way of using language can be seen in Ainscow and Tweddle's (1979) *Preventing Classroom Failure* and Kiernan, Jordan and Saunders (1978) *Starting Off.* The former is particularly concerned with those termed to have 'moderate learning difficulties' and was most influential in helping teachers to see positive ways to achieving steps of learning goals which could be quantified and controlled. The latter was concerned with those termed to have 'severe learning difficulties' and provided a series of play activities that could be systematically taught to children however severely educationally limited they were perceived to be. *Starting Off* became part of my life history during the period of its gestation, as the authors came to do their research for the book at the school at which I taught, using as their subjects the pupils in my 'special care' department. Through this process I observed the transition from a vocabulary of 'caring' to one of 'training'. The researchers proved, through detailed recording of individual progress, that it was possible to train pupils with what were perceived as 'profound and multiple disabilities' to complete simple tasks. They used behaviour modification techniques: rewarding success with food and hugs; punishing failure with loss of attention. To teachers in this school, the emergence of a vocabulary of achievement through modifying behaviour was highly influential. For many, it made a significant difference to their practice.

The Benefits

The benefits of an established *language of mastery of skills* were that teachers, working in this area, no longer felt that they were caring for the ineducable. Despite the change of legislation, turning what were called Junior Training Centres into schools for pupils with severe learning difficulties, there was no significant change in teacher attitude and practice until a new vocabulary had been found. This was provided by texts such as *Preventing Classroom Failure* and *Starting Off*. Many others were published around the late 1970s and early 1980s, which offered detailed individual learning programmes based around 'core skills'. The word 'core' took on a specific meaning in special schools where it was often treated with a reverence otherwise reserved for examination subjects. 'Where is Jane in her core skills?' became as significant in this linguistic context as 'How many GCSEs does Jane have?' would be in the mainstream setting. 'Core skills' could include washing, dressing, feeding, playing, eye-contact, response to verbal communication, going to the toilet: all the multiplicity of elements that reflect being human.

I feel this, in itself, is highly significant. For, in bringing children with profound learning disabilities into an educational rather than caring context, they are being presented as 'human'. The emphasis upon a vocabulary of 'core skills' needs to be understood in relation to this recognition of their humanity. In the recent past, they had been seen as less than human and medical texts had supported this assumption with their graduation of levels of intellectual capacity. Where individuals fell below a specific IQ level they were deemed to be no longer fully human, and were subsequently vulnerable to less than humane treatment. As Bender said,

> Until the late 1960's, the majority of severely and profoundly retarded individuals were immediately institutionalized. The programmes offered for these individuals in state or private facilities were minimal. Curricula that appeared to be successful were criticized because of expense and the amount of time needed for implementation. (1976, p. 251)

It was not, therefore, that they were incapable of learning but that they were deemed unworthy of the effort.

The Dangers

The dangers of this new vocabulary of achievement were that it was value-laden and, therefore, open to abuse and distortion. In the nebulous area of 'core skills', or 'social skills' as they came to be termed, who was to decide what behaviours were appropriate and which tasks were worth pursuing? For many of these learners, 'mastering a skill' was an extremely laborious, time-consuming and stressful occupation. Who was to decide which skills were worth the effort of mastering and why? Out of the 'core skills' language emerged a language of what could be termed 'normalization', for it was concerned with preparing learners to be accepted into a 'normal' social life. In this language, certain customs and behaviours were defined as 'normal' and, there-fore, worth the effort of mastering.

An influential example of this new 'mastering of skills' language was to be found in the Copewell Curriculum, developed at the Hester Adrian Research Centre, University of Manchester. It was a six year research programme funded by the Department of Health and Social Security (DHSS) from 1977 to 1983, directly across the period which included the publication and impact of the Warnock Report. This project aimed to help staff in Adult Training Centres work more effectively with the trainees to aid their 'successful functioning in the Community' (Whelan, Speake and Strickland, 1984, p. 83). As with the transforma-tion of Junior Training Centres from social service care to educational institutions, so Adult Training Centres, at this dramatic period of change, were becoming more educationally aware. 'Special *educational* needs' were influencing the language of training. 'Social skills' were presented, for example, as a series of sequentially graded tasks to be mastered and built upon. Technique had replaced casual spontaneity.

Among the 'core skill' tasks was to know how far away to stand from someone while speaking to them and how much eye-contact to make:

> *18.3 Spatial behaviour*
> is aware of appropriate distance to maintain when inter-
> acting with another individual or individuals.
> *18.4 Visual contact*
> is aware of acceptable eye contact and makes appropriate
> use of eye contact in social interactions.
> (Whelan, Speake and Strickland, 1984, p. 96)

We are now all too aware of the cultural context of social behaviours to accept so rigidly defined a concept of normality. What is useful for us to reflect upon is that such behaviours as these were indicators of the legacy of patronage in the language of special needs. These were people who, as recipients of charity, had to learn to be 'civilized' and subservient. They were being 'normalized' into their place in society, which was one of compliance and useful occupation. If we turn to the language of the 1800s we can more fully understand this legacy.

Despite the evident benefits of applying an educational approach to work in centres, where expectations were often very low, there was the dilemma of imposing establishment values. As I indicated, my analysis of the 'special educational needs' language is that it is paternalistic and complacent. This is illustrated in the language of the Copewell Curriculum. The guidance on 'acceptable' behaviours demonstrates the level of conforming to a rigidly eurocentric, middle-class and restrained model of performance.

Language of Patronage

Disability has long been associated with the shame and stigma of pauperism. In conjunction with this label of dependency comes the need for spiritual sustenance. We have only to turn to the London charities of the 1800s to learn the language of patronage. 'The disabled' equate with 'the damned' as requiring salvation from themselves. In relation to charities for 'the blind and the deaf and dumb':

> The peculiar benefit attached to the charities for instructing these afflicted classes is that such training and instruction call into action other powers, of body and mind, which they may hitherto have been unable to exercise; afford active and useful employment for hours which would otherwise be spent only in gloom and despondency; and prevent that aggravation of suffering which those who endure such peculiar deprivation often experience, viz., the humiliating idea that they are useless in themselves, and a burden to others. (Sampson Low, 1850, pp. 179–80)

There is an overriding emphasis on the need to be (usefully) occupied and to avoid being seen as nothing more than a burden.

The language of patronage does not apply only to the way in which disability was seen to equate with poverty, degradation and despair but extends to the benefactors themselves and their particular status. The London charities of the 1800s were overwhelmingly supported by members of the British Establishment: the 'National Industrial Home for Crippled Boys', for example, had as its President the 'Earl of Meath'; 'The Hospital for Diseases of the Skin' had as patroness the 'Princess of Wales'; and, the 'National Orthopaedic Hospital (for the

Deformed)' had as patron the 'Duke of Cambridge' (Lane, 1887). We now have a charity such as Mencap with a patroness in the form of the Queen Mother and Lord Rix as Chair. We also have the language of 'special educational needs' and the, now, Baroness Warnock.

The Warnock Model

Whilst Dame Mary Warnock, now Baroness Warnock, could not (glibly) be equated with the royal and aristocratic patrons of the 1800s, there are surely some parallels in status and patronage. It is interesting to reflect that in relation to the education of 'handicapped children' who were generally accorded low status, an eminent Oxbridge figure should be selected to chair a committee of enquiry. This is because the power and influence of the British establishment, in all aspects of administrative policy, is pervasive and overwhelming. This establishment lends weight and authority, brings with it centuries of historical legacy, and has the overriding confidence of those who are comfortable and familiar with possessing the right values to impart to others: the voice of enlightened modernity.

What is undeniable is the fact that the Warnock Report, when published in 1978 after several years preparation, made a lasting and dramatic impact upon attitudes and provision. It has also changed the language of special needs. What had, for years, been a predominantly medical model of terminology, with language such as 'idiot', 'cretin', 'moron' replaced by 'educationally sub-normal' and 'maladjusted', 'deaf and dumb' and 'epileptic' — the medical label always coming before the subject — was, at last, discarded. The terms 'special needs', and, specifically, 'special educational needs', was about what the subject experienced — placed after them — rather than defining who or what they were. This language was practical, not just diagnostic. It was no longer the language of a medical consultant:

> He is a hopeless case. They never reach beyond the level of a three year old. Forget him and have another.

This crude parody, whilst offering a caricature of medical patronage, is illustrative of the most extreme examples of practice which 'enlightened modernity' was now challenging in the late 1970s. It is significant to examine the parallel developments in the use of a new language of 'special needs', the growth of new teaching and learning strategies in special and mainstream schools, and the birth of a new level of optimism about the nature of our education system as an inclusive environment for a diversity of participants (e.g., in the work of Booth, Swann and Potts, 1982).

Working in a special school at the time of the influence of 'enlightened modernity' I became aware of how 'special educational needs' was changing teachers. They no longer saw children as 'hopeless'. If they could find the right educational programme, they could then train any child in some skill. This attitude extended to children with difficult behaviour — if the right behaviour modification programme could be found, the behaviour could be checked. Sometimes, this was a frustrating process, full of false starts and experiences of failure, but often it resulted in surprising results. One girl, I recall, after years of hitting her head on walls and floors, was trained in a couple of months to get attention through other means and the destructive behaviour went. This sort of example was immensely gratifying to staff as well as to the pupil. We learnt that we could educate in a purposeful way, instead of just being 'carers'.

In a reflection on my career at this stage (Corbett, 1993) I recorded that the caring role became complex and highly skilled as we were learning to learn from our students — the concept of 'special *educational* needs' was very important to us. We were engaged in a process of 'education', an unfamiliar concept for those in schools for pupils with severe learning difficulties in the early 1970s, burdened as they were with the legacy of social services-run Junior Training Centres. It took until the late 1970s and the language of 'special educational needs' to make these establishments really feel like schools.

One of the most powerful influences of the Warnock Report was to destroy the old divisions between categories of 'handicap', which always fostered an invisible demotion below the 'educable' line, and to replace these with 'special educational needs'. It is common practice today to criticize this term as too diffuse and nebulous to offer any useful purpose of definition. However, we must not forget that it rescued some categories from the *ineducable* mire they might have lingered in. Whilst it is my intention to make the main substance of this book a critique upon 'enlightened modernity', I would be unwise to suggest that much that was good did not emerge from this period of new 'special' language. The focus upon 'educational' obstacles was a welcome change from the 'within-child' deficits of a medical model.

Where I want to challenge the voice of enlightened modernity, in relation to 'special' language, is in its assumptions that there is one right approach to conceptualizing 'need', that this one voice has the authority to speak on behalf of other voices who are kept silent, and that there may not be many forms of language which will take us into new and exciting expressions and imagery and away from 'special needs'. What I certainly feel conscious of at present is that we are locked into a process of struggle to break away from a terminology which, enlightened as it may have been in 1978, now weighs us down with its leaden constrictions.

Conclusion

In this first chapter, I have introduced the voice of enlightened modernity as it relates to the language of special needs. This is the voice of a dominant discourse which is associated with power, status and a confident authority. It is also — despite its enlightened approach in discarding past concepts and out-dated language — a discourse of the status quo, offering a restricted perception of dominant norms and retaining a significant degree of patronage.

Consequently, it is a language which soon atrophies. 'Special educational needs' in the mid-1990s is a redundant term, redolent with oblique undertones of exclusion and stigmatization. Yet we seem to find ourselves unable to change it. Why is this so? How do we foster a new language? Is it necessary to have one dominant discourse or should there be a plurality of diverse discourses — different language for defining specific contexts? Is the retention of *any* kind of special language useful to us anymore? In the following chapters, I hope to explain these issues further and to analyse which voices are emerging and why.

Text 1

Equality Fifteen Years On

Committees of enquiry are on the whole strange creatures, partly innovative, partly following sheep-like where civil servants lead. This committee, of which I was chairman, was no exception. We did not know at the time quite what we were doing, because, as soon as we started to look into it, so many problems arose in the matter of educating children with handicaps in vast variety, temporary or permanent, that our task seemed overwhelmingly hard. But in the end what arose out of this committee, by genuine consensus, was a belief that education was a track along which **every** child and adult had a right to walk, **a right of way**. For some it was a relatively smooth and easy track, for other it was set about with obstacles. These might arise from a variety of causes, and might in some cases be terribly daunting. It was the duty of the education service, we thought, to enable children as far as possible to progress along this track, by helping them to overcome the obstacles. To provide such help was to provide for those children's **special needs**. And thus the concept of educational needs, always latent in educational thinking, and certainly by no means new, came to have prominence in the late 1970s and early 1980s, and was incorporated in the 1981 Education Act. (Warnock, M. (1991) *Oxford Review of Education*, **17**, 2, pp. 145–54)

Questions

1 These are Warnock's reflections on the 1978 language and concepts. Which aspects of this discourse demonstrate the voice of enlightened modernity?
2 Where do the dangers lie in the image of '**a** right of way' (my emphasis)?
3 Define 'special needs' in relation to the above use of language.

2 Different Tracks and Distinct Boundaries

Introduction

If the voice of the British establishment, in the form of the Warnock Report and its subsequent influence, represents enlightened modernity then the dominant discourses of special needs represent different tracks and distinct boundaries. Unless we recognize the distinction of these discourses and their often conflicting perspectives, we are unable to realize why the language of special needs has developed into an obtuse and confusing maze.

Whilst there may be many tracks that I could explore, I have selected what I perceive as four major discourses in special language. To a certain extent these reflect a chronological progression in awareness and increased knowledge. They also demonstrate the impact of partisan views, experiences and mind-maps. These discourses illustrate the now widely held understanding that different groups create their own use of language. Whilst theorists such as Foucault have been related to many areas of education and medicine, Fulcher is one of the few writers who has applied a theory of discourses to the language of special needs. She establishes four main discourses on disability: 'medical, lay, charity and rights discourse' (1989, p. 26). She adds that:

> A fifth discourse, a corporate approach, has begun to emerge: 'managing disability' is one of its themes and its institutional base is emerging among professionals in government welfare agencies and, increasingly, in the private sector in rehabilitation companies. These discourses inform practices in modern welfare states and variously compete or combine to constitute legislative decision, report writing, educational and other practices. (*ibid.*)

Fulcher applies her analysis of distinct disability discourses to an evaluation of government policy, specifically relating to integration in education.

With reference to Fulcher's earlier analysis, I shall explore the four tracks I have selected by examining the use of language and metaphor rather than by relating discourses to policy. My interest, whilst different from hers, is informed and stimulated by her opening up of a neglected area. Special education is rarely exposed to a critical analysis of discourses: the emphasis tends rather to be on practice and models which are seen to be effective. The four discourses which I shall explore in relation to the use of special language are:

1   Psychology
2   Sociology
3   Philosophy
4   Politics

To exclude the medical discourse from this list may appear to be a serious omission but my reasons for doing so are that it is an influence that permeates all of the languages of special needs. I would term the medical discourse as the first stage of enlightened modernity with the voice of Warnock as the second stage. The language of the medical establishment was supplanted but not eradicated by the language of the educational establishment. The specific discourses which I wish to examine are those which form a series of routes or tracks forged by these two stages of enlightened modernity. Out of the formation of several distinctive tracks have been created boundaries which interconnect at certain points but which are also responsible for defensive protection measures to preserve power and status.

In this chapter I shall be introducing the concepts of professional language versus the language used by disabled people themselves. These two areas are not necessarily incompatible, there being a growing body of disabled theorists in 'special needs' subject disciplines whose experiences help to inform their conceptualization of disability. Among those British disabled writers whose ideas are particularly influential in the debate on the language of special needs are Oliver (1992a), Abberley (1987), Shakespeare (1993), French (1992) and Morris (1992), with Begum (1994) and McDonald (1994) offering a dimension of broadening the cultural context. Hevey (1992) is of particular interest in having made a detailed analysis of the use of language and visual imagery in representations of disability. American disabled academics like historian Paul Longmore (e.g., 1986) and cartoonists like Callahan (e.g., reproduced in Shapiro, 1993, p. 17) reflect the political and civil rights approach to disability issues, in which America may be seen to lead Britain in terms of legislation and changing attitudes.

Psychology

This discourse of psychology, closely associated with the medical discourse at its inception, preceded that of sociology and philosophy. As Wright recorded at the first International Conference of the Association for Special Education,

> The first school psychological service in this country was set up over 50 years ago when Cyril Burt was appointed psychologist to the London County Council. His brief was to bring the new skills of a developing psychology which was experimental and biological in outlook, to the problems which arose in an education authority. (1966, p. 207)

One of Burt's key tasks was to discover 'the commonest and the most influential causes of educational backwardness' (Burt, 1952, p. 36), using a degree of precision comparable to medical diagnosis. For all the scientific language applied to educational psychology, the use of metaphor is revealingly ambiguous. In his attempt to define what he perceived by the term 'backwardness', Burt wrote:

> The definitely normal merge through the border-line cases into the definitely sub-normal, much as daylight merges through twilight into night. (1952, p. 37)

This use of poetic imagery is far from scientific or objective and its use as a means of definition which categorizes and decides educational futures seems bizarre. He goes on to admit that the definition of backwardness 'must necessarily be somewhat arbitrary, based on practical convenience or convention, like the hour fixed for lighting up' (*ibid.*). In the use of such metaphors, Burt indicates how hazardous a process of definition this procedure was and how easily it could be prone to error.

It is worth reflecting on the ambiguous nature of 'backwardness' or 'educational subnormality' or 'slow learners' or 'moderate learning difficulty'. This sequential labelling process of a nebulous category of special need, always comprising the most substantial section, has developed from a 'twilight' conceptualization of 'lighting up' times. As Burt noted, according to convenience (i.e., how many places there were to be filled in special schools; how many mainstream schools needed to get rid of troublesome pupils) and convention (what was perceived to be 'backward' at that time, in that city, by that headteacher, in the view of that educational psychologist), 'lighting up' times (i.e., cut-off lines delineating normal and subnormal categories) would be decided. The use of 'twilight' imagery conveys a sense of mystery, obtuseness and fear of the on-coming dark. It is the imagery of special needs which I discussed in the introduction: combining elements of sentimentality and fear. Normality is flooded with light (symbolizing righteousness and clarity) whilst those souls on the borderline slip towards darkness (symbolizing evil and confusion). As a voice of enlightened modernity, Burt represents the power to select a 'lighting up' time based on his superior judgment in the face of evident indecision.

Whilst it may seem patently obvious that theorists of the 1950s would have different conceptions of education than those of the 1990s, it is important that we reflect on the legacy of our special educational practice and the way in which language was employed. There is often an almost reverential attention given to the assessments that educational psychologists offer. But their use of professional jargon and specific criteria does not automatically make their judgment correct. In a recent research evaluation of the effectiveness of such assessments, Galloway, Armstrong and Tomlinson (1994) suggest that conflict and confusion can result from a lack of clear policy from Local Education Authorities (LEAs) and schools. In 1994, these authors state that the concept of Special Educational Need (SEN) is still 'shrouded in ambiguity' and 'hopelessly confused'. What seems to be crucial in evaluating the impact of the psychology 'track' on special language, is to recognize that those who decide the 'lighting up' times are influenced by many external factors. In some circumstances, the lights will be turned on early and those caught in the twilight are exposed to their glare. At other times, the lights will only be turned on at the last possible moment, to conserve resources, thus leaving more individuals to roam freely (or, at risk) in the twilight. This metaphor is the science of defining what constitutes 'backwardness'.

Sociology

One of the key sociological discourses established in Britain and of international influence is that created by the work of Tomlinson (e.g., 1981; 1982). She made us examine the language we habitually use, explore how what Fulcher (1989) terms 'a corporate approach' is established, and question the way in which certain children become labelled, categorized and destined for different schooling. The status of special education was an aspect of the sociological discourse which particularly interested me. In her analysis, Tomlinson suggested that there were distinct layers of educational 'tracks', each carrying a different status. The top layer was private and public schooling; privileged and commanding high status. The middle layer was mainstream schooling; where 'normal' children attended. The bottom layer was special schooling; least desirable and lowest status.

The sociological discourse creates a conflicting boundary with the psychological discourse. Educational psychologists were supposed to *help* a child by finding an appropriate placement. The sociological language translates this 'help' into a 'betrayal'. It is particularly interesting to reflect on how a sociological analysis of the use of special language can challenge the voice of enlightened modernity in its two elements: both Warnock and the legacy of defining 'cut-off' points, left by Burt. Galloway *et al.* suggest that:

> Each of the three words *special, educational* and *needs* raises its own questions. 'Special' is defined in the Oxford dictionary as: 'of a peculiar or restricted kind'. While that may be true of children with severe and complex difficulties, it is obviously not true of the mainstream school pupils to whom the term could be applied. As we have just argued, Warnock extended the term to include the large minority of underachieving and mainly working-class pupils whose education became politically contentious with the economic changes in the late 1970s. Far from being special, there is a powerful argument that the children's needs were absolutely normal, and that the challenge for the school system was, quite simply, to start meeting them. (1994, p. 14)

Whereas the language of psychology is one which distinguishes the parts that veer from the perceived 'norm', that of sociology redefines the boundaries of what constitutes 'normality'. What these authors conclude in their analysis is that the 'special needs pupil' discourse is essentially individualistic, attributing learning difficulties to factors in the pupil's family and social background' (1994, p. 16). Where I feel that a philosophical discourse is of particular value is that it moves away from the individual and the particular (the 'case study' model so prevalent in special education) towards an exploration of language, imagery and the values behind thoughts and words.

Philosophy

Booth (1988) challenges our concept of equal worth by asking whether we really consider a learner who gains Oxbridge entrance to be of no more value than someone who has learning disabilities. 'Equal opportunities' and 'entitlement' are much abused terms. They are usually qualified by 'if resources allow', 'when conditions are suitable' and 'where appropriate'. The economic and social inequalities which foster different educational tracks, ensure that more value is placed on a select few and that we soon learn which strata we fit. Booth quotes Warnock's 1985 Dimbleby lecture, remarking of teachers who consider strike action:

> Teachers on strike get little sympathy, however reasonable their case: and they do their image irreparable harm. They are thought to put themselves on a level with other wage-earners — miners, car workers, and those whose jobs are concerned with the production of goods. (Warnock, 1985, p. 10, quoted in Booth, 1988, p. 118)

As Booth reflects, what does this say about Warnock's attitude to those in the kinds of employment which she clearly considers 'trade' rather than 'professional'; let alone her concept of people with learning disabilities.

It seems important to me that we consider these attitudes, expressed by a philosopher, and that we ask the kind of provocative questions that Booth asks. If the voice of enlightened modernity, as exemplified by Warnock and reflected in the establishment values, is a voice which is speaking of 'integration' of 'children with special needs', where does it see that integration taking place?

One of the key concerns among educationalists over recent years has been the way in which integration has often been so narrowly interpreted. The most easily assimilated pupils were the first to be integrated, those whose disabilities created minimal challenge to the existing system. The notion of 'a right to walk' along a single 'track' was reflected in the struggle for a more integrated school community. Schools are inflexible for many learners and the prevailing ethos, fostered by current government initiatives in Britain, means that the track is getting narrower and more confining. 'Integration' has come to mean the following in all but the most exceptional of situations: adapt to what exists; do not ask for extra resources; become like the majority; conceal your difficulties; learn to fit in. Numerous accounts of the individual experiences of pupils with disabilities testify to the traumas and suffering of assimilation at all costs, denying the reality of differences.

Brouillette suggests that there is a new era ahead of us:

> The *third stage* of social development emerging in the beginning of the 21st century could be characterised by a higher regard and tolerance for the rights of an individual to be different; to be disabled. (1993, p. 253)

If this prediction is to be believed, the mood to support a change in behaviour can only be created by the disability movement, building a political force which can no longer be ignored.

Politics

The major political voice of the disability movement has emerged as Oliver's (1990), in his clarification of the key elements of the disability political front. He traces the development of the disability movement in five stages:

partnership/patronage;
economic/parliamentarian;
consumerist/self-help;
populist/activist;
umbrella/coordinating.

In his analysis, the use of language is of particular significance. The crucial words are powerful prepositions: very small but powerful in their emphasis. The first two stages are 'for' disabled people whilst the latter three are 'of' disabled people. Oliver contends, therefore, that only these three latter organizations can constitute a new social movement as they are truly empowered and unrestrained by patronage or the compromise of an uneasy partnership.

I think that the emphasis within the disability movement on a word like 'of' and a distinct rejection of 'for' is reflective of the perennial tensions which exist between those (teachers, academics, researchers, charity organizers, carers, nurses) who work 'for' and the political movements 'of' disabled people. If we consider the national picture and the voices of the 'silent majority' of disabled people, it is safe to assume that non-disabled people working on their behalf is a given which is largely unchallenged and often welcomed. The disability movement, like any radical political group, is reflective of minority views within the disabled community and will polarize opinions in its call to action. What I find particularly exciting, in relation to the development of language and the introduction of new metaphors, is that this social movement has found a range of clear voices, speaking for themselves and for the cause of disability rights.

Morris (1991), as a disabled feminist and a most articulate and courageous writer, explores a wide range of political issues including the right to life. She wants to give value to the lives of all disabled people, recognizing that this involves fostering positive attitudes among those who work 'for' disabled people. The language that she employs always gives dignity and value to disabled people, placing their right to be treated as significant citizens alongside the rights of other minority groups.

In my comparison of the disability movement and gay pride (Corbett, 1994b), I suggest that in both political groups there is an impetus to replace the language of stigma with the language of pride. A valuable tool in this transformation is the power of solidarity that peer support provides. This sharing of feelings, needs and experiences can act as a catalyst for change, at both an individual and collective level.

Hevey conveys this strength of the collective in the use of mystical metaphors. He speaks of the silencing of his references to his experience of epilepsy:

> Each time I 'came out', similar responses of silencing occurred. I was in a double bind because, although I was filled with a chaotic rage when they pushed my coming out back down my throat, I felt myself capitulate to their silencing of myself as a disabled person because I too wished 'it' were dead and silent. Despite the attempts and the guises, I was brought back, once again, to my great unpronounceable fear that dare not speak its name. Once again, I had tried to reinvent most parts of myself but I could not reinvent the burning core of my self, the epilepsy and disablement. It was time to meet the dread. I found and joined the disability movement. The journey into the valley had ended and the journey out of the valley begun. (1992, p. 78)

Hevey's 'conversion' from shame to pride and a 'coming out' into acknowledging his comparatively hidden disability is graphically drawn. Then, using the language of spiritual transformation 'out of the valley of darkness was I led', he conveys something of the immense significance of this experience for him as an individual. He then moves on to use a literary analogy. He suggests that much political theorizing remains objective, whereas he wanted to move to the subjective:

> Miranda stood on dry ground observing the shipwreck. I gave up the Miranda syndrome and admitted my own wreckage. (*ibid.*)

Taking an international signifier like Shakespeare and comparing his former stance to that of Miranda in *The Tempest*, Hevey is bringing the language of special needs into a mainstream cultural arena. Whilst this may seem exaggerated and even pretentious in its inference, the placing of 'special' language into a context of high culture locates it at the heart of human experience. I feel this is an important stage in the evolution of special language as it moves it from a purely applied location (linked to professional jargon and, thus, speaking to a restricted audience) into a central arena which uses a universal discourse. This literary metaphor, linking disability to universal human experience, moves special language out of a ghetto status into the centre. In doing this, the language leaves 'for', behind, embraces 'of', and gathers momentum. Hevey describes this in mystical and magical terms:

> People were coming out of physical or psychic prisons into a powerful personal and political light. The energy is and was extraordinary. Of course, what I and others were bearing witness to was the living political transformation of the medical model of disablement into the social model of disablement. It was this magic and transformation that I begun to photograph. (1992, p. 79)

One of the distinctive features of this assertive energy, found in all groups that seek an identity which fosters their proud image, is in its focus on artistic expression. Whether it is in photography or art, sculpture or dance, acting or singing, disability arts has become a definite part of the new language of a political movement that seeks a wide audience and which supports diverse voices celebrating the joy of difference.

Different Tracks and Distinct Boundaries

In my concluding section to this chapter, I want to reflect on the range of 'tracks' and 'boundaries' which have been discussed and compared.

The 'track' of psychology may be seen as a successor to the medical model, supporting an approach which seeks to categorize and assess, measuring always against a defined 'norm'. The 'sociology' track questions that concept of 'norm' setting 'special needs' into a context of class, race, gender and sexuality. It breaks away from boundaries of psychological measurement but, in the process, creates its own boundary of subjective analysis of social groups. The 'philosophical' track presents an ethical and civil rights approach to 'special needs' questioning values and humanity, integrity and truth. It erodes boundaries created by professionals who defend their territories of power and status. It challenges notions of 'expertise'. To some extent, I see the philosophical discourse, with its focus upon the use of language, metaphor and imagery as paving the way to a new use of words, a new ownership of the language of disability and a move towards deconstructing the power of earlier discourses.

For the second text in this book, I have selected an example which is a dramatic contrast with the voice of enlightened modernity heard in Text 1. It offers a striking illustration of the contribution that disability arts has already made in Britain and the USA. The author shows how empowering are the words and images created by disabled artists and performers. She also indicates that there are many voices, forging many tracks and that all have a right to be heard and valued.

Text 2

Searching for Disability Arts

I was looking for disability arts. Coming from a socialist background and the feminist and gay liberation movements I felt sure there'd be a political analysis of disability. Art can express politics in a powerful way.

I asked librarians, 'Where are your books about disability?' They looked puzzled. 'Do you mean about aids and things?' 'No. I mean about the way society treats disabled people, about people's attitudes.' They didn't know what I was talking about.

Then I found the Greater Manchester Coalition for Disabled People and my first item of disability arts, **Ian Stanton's** *Shrinking Man* tape. It was a good day. I love that mixture of humour, political clout and creativity in Ian's songs. 'Got a chip on your shoulder/ a real bad attitude/ is it any wonder people treat you the way they do?/ You really should be grateful for all we try and do for you/ and be a quiet little crip without a chip.' Well, is he good at sing-along, community-building ditties, or what? Guess it depends on whether you agree with him. I wrote a gushing fan letter; Ian was modest and warm in reply.

I scoured television and radio listings. I sent for everything possible about disability politics and disability arts. I went to see **David Hevey's** *The Creatures Time Forgot* photographic exhibition in Bradford. I was very excited because so many issues were addressed by his work. I enjoyed the mixture of gender, race, sexuality, visible/invisible impairments. I was particularly overjoyed by a photograph of two lesbians. It was a great photograph; proud, joyful, relevant. I would love that picture on my wall. It adds to my feeling good about being a disabled lesbian.

Soon after this I had telephone contact with a couple of women in **No Excuses** theatre cabaret which had a big effect on me. I was proud they were an all-woman team and whenever I saw them on TV. I felt elated. I love their way of getting serious political ideas across by taking the piss. I felt the way they worked collectively, co-operatively, supportively with each other showed on stage. I like their decision to only perform at accessible venues.

I came into contact with **Sue Napolitano's** poetry in June

1991 and was impressed. She's strong, clear and funny. She rabble-rouses and tackles tender, intimate, personal experiences. She's positive, witty and acute. Sue is a powerful performer, who gently takes an audience by the scruff, gets them on her side and somehow gets us chanting 'Break the Rules'.

Sue uses experiences from her own life and analyses them. Take her monologue about the struggle to fulfil her 'latest wild idea' — to bathe independently. A salesman 'dripping with sales patter' takes the bath (which won't fit through the front door) into her back garden. She has to put up with 'ho-ho jokes' about people passing on a Number 11 bus and him saying he wants to be a guest at the party when she finally gets in. However, Sue remarks dryly, 'It is important to be polite when you're disabled, you know.'

The non-disabled salesman is rude and invasive, asking, like so many others, for an explanation of her life story. However, Sue needs his information because the woman who usually lifts her in and out of the bath is pregnant (and Sue doesn't want her to have a miscarriage!).

The bath Sue needs costs £2000 (typical rip off). She laments the age it takes to get an assessment by the Social Services and that if they decide it's not needed — 'after all, they're the experts' — Sue would be faced with trying to raise £2000.

Sue delivers this monologue with so much irony and humour it is impossible for her audience not to be on her side. Yet the political points are delivered with serious impact. As Sue concludes, 'This is the sort of thing you have to put up with if you're disabled and want to take a bath.' Disabled people can identify with her and non-disabled people (if they're open to it) learn a lot.

Sue's poetry is personal and political, a combination I find powerful. When a non-disabled person comments over her head, 'Hasn't she got a lovely smile?' Sue replies, 'I can curl my lip and snarl', throwing in for good measure that she 'has had hairy armpits for over twenty years'. The staccato rhythm in this poem is the craft which conveys her anger and distaste, her art is in direct accessible language which fits her theme.

'I hear you snigger when I say "Hump",' Sue begins another poem in a low, 'Gothic' voice. 'To be straight is to be good', she tells us, summing up with lovely irony a whole ethos of our society. In challenging this stricture Sue is courageously vulnerable. She states how long she kept her body hidden in swathes of clothes, how long it took her to wear a swimming costume in public and to say the word 'hump'. She now asserts, 'This body is where I live my life.'

I could go on with more examples of Sue's punchy, ironic handling, her appropriate rhythm, intonation, accurate choice of words, metaphors, images, the way she takes you into the atmosphere of a scene in a couple of lines.

A piece of visual art which has affected me greatly appeared in DAM #3/2. *Viva* by **Gioya Steinke** had an immediate and lasting impact. This striving body (sex indeterminate) fills me with myriad emotion. Struggle, joy, searching, celebration. This picture has replayed itself inside my head in so many situations and never fails to uplift me. A contributor to DAIL once lamented the lack of form in Gioya's work. For me this picture lacks nothing and gives so much. Thank you, Gioya.

I'm aware I'm not balancing this article with contributors from every discipline and it is difficult to concentrate on a few examples of disability art as I have been affected by so many. However, I must convey some idea of how I have been opened, thrilled and jarred by the performance work, poetry and stories of **Char March**.

Char (pronounced Shar) was the first person to offer me an alternative terminology for psychiatric illness by announcing she has mental distress. As someone who in my late teens and early twenties was pumped full of myriad psychiatric drugs, some of which have since been banned, it was a term with which I could identify. It took away the stigma and feeling of failure and stated a reality.

Char is an entertaining, outrageous and dramatic performer, a great ad-lib artist. She can be loud, expansive, daring but isn't afraid to drag in abysmal, swampy pain. She's a professional, who works to make an impact and seeks feedback to improve. She's open to the views of others but she's not afraid to challenge.

I've seen her draw in a lesbian audience with a cosy tale of how heterosexual people are often unable to accept she is a lesbian: 'You treated me like a disease/ a horrifying abnormality/ as sad/ as a threat/ as sick/ frightening/ disgusting . . .' Next moment we are confronted by her addressing lesbians who cannot accept her madness: 'You have withdrawn/ backed out of seeing me . . . / You treat me like a timebomb'. Making people feel uncomfortable is a dangerous way to get across political ideas — the defensiveness can be boring — but amongst the shuffling and squirming I'm sure intellectual light bulbs pop on.

Lesbians can be wary of the 'sick' or 'crazy' interpretation of our sexuality, falling over backwards 'trying to be most perfect/ and balanced/ thoroughly nice human being who-just-happens-to-be-a-lesbian'. Char is a self-styled crazy lesbian. For lesbians who have mental distress this unapologetic, matter of fact treatment is long overdue.

Char states, 'It is dangerous to come out as lesbian, or to come out as mad. It is doubly dangerous to come out as both. I realise the power of this explosive mix.' Char turns this power like a search-light on us all and refuses to be silenced and crushed.

Char also tackles sexual, physical, emotional abuse and self-harm: 'A bleeding hand is so much easier to focus on, bandage, heal, cosset, feel compassion for than a ripped apart mind'. It takes courage to bring these things into the open. Char has tremendous courage.

Char doesn't abide by the rules. She is not polite. If Char doesn't like what's happening there is no escape: 'I want to be an iceberg/ to gash/ an unstoppable hole/ in their complacency'.

Her distress ain't pretty: she's a 'sob-bag', her tears 'splop' on the carpet, 'frayed nerve endings hang in fringes', her throat 'feels like a rusty fish-hook', she scrubs wallpaper clean of lies, throws a mug through a window, opens her mouth 'wide until my jaw aches' with screams 'I can now/ suddenly/ no longer be bothered to scream'. 'Writing and performing are,' she says, 'main factors in keeping me well, happy and alive'. In a performance piece for Survivor's Poets Char tells us: 'through the ache/ paper and pen materialise/ strange keys to the door. . . .'

Char is also funny, generous, warm, refreshing, elevating. I find these lines intoxicating: 'sometimes I dance the thin line/ whirling in the sun/ shouting in an arms-up, head-back laugh/ this/ is my life/ out here/ (on this edge)/ a slim chance/ with steep drops on either side,/ but Christ the views/ are bloody marvellous.'

'Life, not existence,' says Char, 'is what I aim for.' I second that emotion. (Alison Silverwood (1994) *Disability Arts Magazine*)

Questions

1   Discuss the examples of how disability arts have 'opened, thrilled and jarred' Alison Silverwood's mind. What particular qualities does she see in them?

2 How does she link disability politics with other forms of oppression? What is the impact of this?

3 Discuss the power in a line like 'Life, not existence, is what I aim for'. How does it reflect movements 'of' rather than 'for' disabled people?

3   Deconstructing Special Language

Introduction

In an attempt to apply a postmodernist analysis to special language, I suggest that:

> The potential value of deconstructing the medical and educational assumptions upon which special needs has been built is that it necessitates a new way of viewing multiple realities and a way of listening to previously unheard discourses. (Corbett, 1993, p. 549)

In this chapter I shall compare the existing strata of 'special needs' discourses with potential alternatives. The strengths and weaknesses of a process of deconstruction will be evaluated. I am asking three questions:

1   Why do we need to deconstruct?
2   What is the value of this process?
3   Where do the risks lie?

My analysis is founded on the assumption that Warnock is the voice of enlightened modernity, offering a new way forward from the old models of special educational terminology but presenting restricted ways of defining 'integration'. Whilst the imagery and language that has developed over the last twenty years can be seen to be an improvement on the old, inevitable limitations and complacencies, they require continual critical reassessment.

1   Why Do We Need to Deconstruct

Language reflects conceptions of reality, or truth. As such, I feel that the term 'special need' is no longer useful or constructive. To me, it is reflective of a professional ownership where medical and educational

Figure 3.1   Deconstructing special languages

| MEDICAL |
| PSYCHOLOGY |
| SOCIOLOGY |
| PHILOSOPHY |
| POLITICS |
| CIVIL RIGHTS |
| DISABILITY ARTS |

(A)

FEMINISM/SEXUALITY	RACE/GENDER/CULTURE	POLITICS/AIDS/SUB-CULTURES	DISABILITY/ARTS/MUSIC/SONG/POETRY	PARENTS/RADICAL PROFESSIONAL-ALLIES	CHILDREN WITH LABELS

(B)

definitions dominate the discourse. It jars uncomfortably with the discourses in the disability movement where new languages and metaphors are emerging in a creative burst of pride and assertion. This creativity has extended to the academic discourse where Oliver (1992) has promoted a new level of collaboration in disability research, ensuring that disabled researchers and subjects are heard and their voices given power and status.

To indicate how I perceive this existing pattern of special language discourses and the potential of a post-deconstruction stage, see Figure 3.1.

In (A) I perceive the dominant discourses of special needs within a layered hierarchy. This sequence is both chronological and denotes a degree of status which still pertains. Despite the academic debates and civil rights movements of disabled people and their allies, the medical model has not been dislodged to any significant degree. Equally, the role of educational psychologists remains dominant in the assessment and educational career of children with 'special educational needs'. I have deliberately constructed this part of the figure as a series of horizontal stages as I suggest that, although there are connecting debates within these discourses, the dominant status of some over the others creates an unequal hierarchy. The likelihood of medical discourses on disability being influenced by the voices in disability arts areas seems improbable. One of the developments which I shall be arguing for in this chapter is the increased cross-fertilization of different discourses to enrich, challenge and change the way in which language is used and created.

In (B) I have presented a series of upright layers of discourses, rather than a horizontal sequence. This is to denote the following aspects of my analysis:

1   That no one voice in these discourses be allowed to dominate;
2   That multi-faceted discourses are heard and given space for expression;
3   That notions of 'special need' and 'disability' are taken out of their formerly restricted areas and brought into contact with a diverse range of related and relevant debates on experiences of marginalization;
4   Above all, that an ever-expanding space be allowed to accommodate new voices which have for too long remained silent or unheard in the clamour for status.

Whereas in (A) the political, civil rights and artistic expression of the disability movement will continue to struggle to be heard within an establishment hierarchy of dominant discourses, in (B) the diversity of voices are of equal status, bringing in many perspectives and celebrating this range of views and expressions.

2   What is the Value of this Process?

For me the value of a deconstruction of existing discourses and a free-for-all in allowing no voice to gain dominance over others is that this process is stimulating, exciting and liberating of itself. Of course, it is frightening to let go of old certainties and to acknowledge that our new dogmas may soon become as imprisoning of ideas as those old dogmas we so vociferously rejected. It requires courage, self-trusting, standing-apart; what Walters terms 'a modestly sceptical and independent approach to judgement' (1994, p. 53). I agree with his recognition that because this process often creates temporary confusion the gaining of independent reasoning is both disconcerting and disorienting, both in relation to the established hierarchies and political allegiances and, more painfully, in relation to oneself. As he emphasizes, an essential ingredient of achieving a critical level of independence of mind is being able to withstand some degree of unease and stress and finding the courage and strength of will to endure the passage. Walters uses a powerful metaphor to describe the significance of this preparation:

To neglect this is to fling potent, costly seeds into desiccated unploughed soil. (*ibid.*)

I feel that we need to learn from such an analogy. Changing the way we use 'special needs' languages; conceptualizing fresh metaphors for disability; bringing marginalized discourses into the centre; reframing ways of listening; fostering unheard debates; relocating old hierarchies; forging new words in multiple arenas: all of this amounts to a frightening, wonderful potential for growth. Yet these 'costly seeds' ('costly' because they are produced through pain and struggle) can only flourish, ripen and reproduce if ploughed into receptive 'soil'. For me, the process of deconstruction, in relation to special language, is about working to prepare that ground, ridding it of all previous traces, churning it up, opening spaces where new seeds can grow unchoked by the layers of earlier sediment.

Language is delicate yet robust, malleable yet fixed. There is a perennial tension when taking ownership of languages in giving permission for voices to be heard. An interesting example of this was illustrated in the 1994 Booker Prize fiasco in Britain during October 1994. In this annual scramble for a literary award, the book which won among the six short-listed authors was an example of a marginalized discourse being placed in the centre. James Kelman's (1994) *How Late It Was, How Late* is a story about a man on the margin of society, drunk, poor, in and out of prison, violent, outcast and disabled by blindness. This author, proud of his Scottish heritage, writes in a dense dialect, both regional and brutal:

> Move it ya fucking pest. This was sodjer number 2 talking; then his hand was on Sammy's right shoulder and Sammy let him have it, a beautiful left cross man he fucking overed him one, right on the side of the jaw, and his fucking hand, it felt like he'd broke it. And sodjer number 1 was grabbing at him but Sammy's foot was back and he let him have it hard on the leg and the guy squeaked and dropped and Sammy was off and running cause one minute more and they would be back at him for christ sake these stupit fucking trainers man his poor auld toe it felt like it was fucking broke it was pinging yin yin poioioioiong. (Kelman, 1994, p. 5)

The language is challenging, aggressive, uncompromising and hard. It requires great concentration of mind to *hear* this language. What Kelman seems to be telling us is that, if we are going to hear marginalized individuals, like his protagonist, then we have to make considerable efforts to *listen*. Some of the Booker Prize judges found such an attitude to be an outrageous affront. They dismissed the book as 'crap', deeming it impenetrable, unreadable and insulting to the average reader. The British tabloid newspapers were quick to take up this rallying cry, with a series of contemptuous leader comments on the nonsense of such texts gaining this level of recognition and exposure. The inference is that what most readers want is a book which uses language we recognize, find easy and can identify with.

I think that the example of the Booker Prize drama is useful as a pointer to where deconstructing special language will meet pitfalls. We feel comfortable with words we know, people that we at least slightly like or can fit to a familiar stereotype, a plot that moves to a traditional pattern. Authors like Kelman can be seen to destroy the old certainties. They break grammatical rules, dismiss the conventional characters and create anarchy in their use of form. The anger and distaste which they initiate is about fear. It is uncomfortable to be thrown into a shapeless muddle of words. Yet, what Kelman seems to be saying is that, for people like his protagonist, life is a formless confusion. Language, therefore, has to reflect this.

3 Where Do the Risks Lie?

Anarchic structures and formless confusion can create chaos. If language is 'up for grabs' and multiple discourses spawned with alarming speed, the resulting brawl is potentially highly destructive. The hierarchies, or 'master narratives' as they are sometimes termed, were constraining and oppressive yet there was comfort in the certainties. Presenting a feminist analysis, Acker says that:

> Grand theories and 'master narratives' are no longer desirable constructions, when knowledge is recognized as provisional, grounded and uncertain. In one sense, this is good news for feminists, because it parallels what their critique has been asserting; in another, it is destabilizing, for surely the feminist alternatives are just as provisional and uncertain. (1994, p. 57)

Here lies the highest risk for all revolutionary discourses. Whilst they are seeking to establish their position in a clearly defined, recognized and respected course, they are as vulnerable as all other alternatives to destruction in the whims of language trends. To a significant extent, such a degree of instability can mitigate against equality of opportunity

Figure 3.2   Deconstructing special language: risks

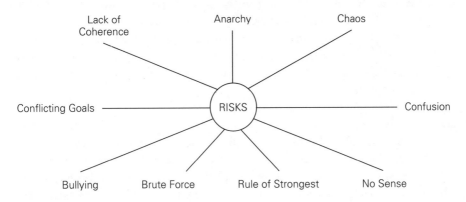

which feminists, black groups, disability rights activists and gay rights groups fear. Where certain voices have fought for their right to come in from the margins and be heard, the knowledge that the centre is now as high-risk and volatile as their formerly marginalized status is threatening to say the least.

This volatility and grappling for a platform creates a climate in which brute force and bullying can flourish. In Figure 3.2, the potential risks of deconstructing special languages are drawn up. If we apply these risks specifically to the use of special language, they can be seen to have the following consequences:

> *Lack of Coherence*, leading to separation in disability groups, each pursuing their own goals, with subsequent loss of power;
> *Anarchy*, creating a scramble for status and a blurring of clarity;
> *Chaos*, in which the reconstruction of special languages or pride and strength has to struggle;
> *Confusion*, as it requires time, concentration and structure to forge new discourses and too many too soon dilutes the reconstructive force;
> *No Sense*, leading to frustration and rejection of new languages, as words have to be found which communicate and connect;
> *Rule of Strongest*, where there is a real danger of more vulnerable sections of the disability movement, perhaps those who lack ease of articulation in particular, being overruled and colonized by stronger groups;
> *Brute Force*, in which new languages will be fought for and the politics of language will result in dominant discourses emerging as victors, whilst others are defeated and made invisible and inaudible;

Bullying, could lead to factions within the special education and medical discourses forcing vulnerable groups to align themselves with these discourses or perish in the confusion;

Conflicting Goals, coming full circle back to 'lack of coherence', where different special discourses have conflicting goals this acts against solidarity and power and encourages infighting and disharmony.

Deconstructing special languages is risky. If we no longer regard medical, psychological and educational discourses on 'special needs' as privileged and open up the area to include the multifaceted disability discourses, there is a risk of the rule of the strongest prevailing. Groups that were strong on their own territory in the margins can easily be destroyed in a competition against much bigger, stronger discourses in the centre.

I would prefer to see this process as a struggle and, ideally, as a means of exchanging ways of understanding and expressing ideas. Taking the example of mental illness, I shall explore recent discourses which have moved from the margins to challenge the centre. People with mental illness may be seen as particularly susceptible to intimidation or coercion and, as such, incapable of establishing new discourses for themselves. This has not proved to be the case, although the discourse I shall explore is far removed from that of psychiatry. In the language of poetry, words and metaphors have deconstructed the old ways of seeing.

Survivors Against the System

'Survivors' Poetry was founded in 1991 by four poets who have had first-hand experience of the mental health system. Peter Campbell, in his introduction to their first anthology, defines the way in which survivors see themselves:

Although we are mad for a season we are marked in perpetuity. The standard response to our distress sets us up beyond society and sets us at odds within ourselves. The challenge we face is to repossess our experience and to reclaim our dignity and value as citizens.

Survivors are not incompetent. Nor are we devoid of insight. Many of the problems we share with other disadvantaged minorities — unemployment, poverty, isolation — are the result of discrimination rather than incapacity. But we need not deny our distress to achieve acceptance. The boundaries of approved experience are narrow enough already.

Through poetry and music, visual arts, writing and action we must fight for a broader understanding, a re-evaluation of individual experience.

Let the struggle continue.

Vive la Difference.

(Campbell, 1992, p. 6)

The affirmative language brings in challenging concepts to discourses on mental illness. It says that it is alright to recognize distress, that boundaries of experiences need broadening and that differences can be valued with an increased level of understanding. Poetry transforms the context of this discourse. Whereas psychiatry has its roots in medical science, research and theoretical hierarchies, poetry is receptive to all shapes and sounds, is open and free from censure. In challenging imagery, it can aid new levels of consciousness and help us to see differently.

Seddon, in relation to the reframing of educational theory, suggests that:

> Moving beyond context means pursuing contextualism by not putting limits on connectedness or falling into what is at issue is not things and concepts and how they are made to change but processes of formation and transformation which are inherently dynamic. (1994, p. 196)

If we apply this analysis to the special needs discourses, it is the processes by which attitudes and behaviours are shaped that determines the contextual developments. New ways of looking can gradually create new contexts, which transform power relations.

The value of using expressive arts in psychiatry has gained increased recognition. Some doctors make effective use of drama, for example, but Holmwood (1994) found, in his investigations, that many doctors were too busy to include such an extension of existing services. One doctor who used drama told him that:

> Many will say, 'Well, I'm so busy dealing with the crocodiles I haven't got time to drain the swamp.' (1994, p. 23)

This metaphor offers a vivid example of why deconstruction in established discourses is so necessary, albeit risky. Crisis management is a feature of much professional practice. Whilst it is inevitably so, under increased pressure and demands, it presents an obstacle to progress. It is only if we can make time to 'drain the swamp' that new approaches can be applied, different strategies explored and unfamiliar dialogues established.

One of these dialogues is between providers of services and their users. This applies at all levels of disability services. In the magazine for Democratic Psychiatry, called *Asylum,* a recent article was on 'understanding Professional Thought Disorder' (PTD). In this deliberate use of professional jargon, users of services challenge providers to look to their behaviour. This challenge is made through the use of professional language, opened up into a critique of practice. Among the examples are the following:

> *What are the signs of PTD?*
> Every person with PTD is unique; however it is useful to know the common symptoms to look for which may indicate the presence of PTD.
> *Inappropriate affect/emotional rigidity*
> . . . a compulsion to analyse and compartmentalise the experiences of others, presumably to protect their own fragility . . .
> *Disordered cognition*
> . . . rigidly held beliefs (which are held to be 'facts'). Such beliefs are not affected by empirical evidence from the real world . . .
> *Delusions of grandeur*
> . . . sufferers tend to see themselves as important, gifted and beneficent . . .
> *Negative transference and projection*
> . . . a common feature is that the sufferer is unable to distinguish their own wishes and impulses from those of people they believe themselves to be helping . . .
> (Lowson, 1994, p. 29)

When the tables are turned in this manner, it demonstrates the degree of paternalism that permeates professional language. It is revealed as a language of rigidity, imperviousness and defensiveness. It is also distinctly sinister.

The use of poetic imagery enables the recipients of professional treatment to express their feelings. Whereas they are alienated and often intimidated by the use of professional jargon and what might be termed the language of categorization, poetry allows them freedom of speech. It forms a powerful means of fighting back. Among the contributions to the *Survivors' Poetry* anthology, for example, is the following:

The Mental Health Rack

You've taken our minds and we want them back
You've put our humanity on your mental health rack
You've stolen our will, you've denied us our rights . . .
Yes, if you should prove difficult, start noticing the cracks
We'll increase the dose and turn the screws
on our mental health rack . . .
(Paulette Ng, 1992, p. 54)

This poem compares psychiatrists to torturers. The professional 'care' is interpreted as malign and dangerous. In many areas of the disability movement, such attitudes now prevail. Professionals are mistrusted. Their 'concern' is treated with caution. Professional guidance often meets with disdain. These grounds for hostility are built on a history of oppression and unequal power relations which can only change slowly, with compromise, humility and respect.

Is There a Way Forward?

Do we need to obliterate the special languages of the past (were this really feasible) and, if not, how can a fruitful dialogue be established? Each discourse, created in the past, represented a 'way forward' from the existing structures. Thus, medicine produced discourses on diagnosis and treatment, moving on from a stage of fear and ignorance relating to disability. Educational psychology forged a discourse of assessment linked to placement, moving on from a dismissal of people as ineducable and untrainable. Sociology and philosophy of special education discourses widened the debates to include context — economic, political and demographic — and the ethical dilemmas surrounding decisions. In this respect, can we not take the most valuable and durable elements of each established special needs discourse and connect these to issues raised in current debates?

The challenge is in reconciling diversity with universality. It is difficult to reconcile diverse and conflicting community values with universal values. Yet, unless there is an attempt to achieve a degree of reconciliation, the resulting confusion defuses force and power to effect necessary changes. An example of this attempt to reconcile different voices in the special needs debates was demonstrated at the British Institute for Learning Disabilities Annual Conference in 1994. This forum brought together medical practitioners, clinical psychologists, social workers, sociologists, care workers, community hospital nurses, people with learning disabilities and their parents. This combination of perspectives resulted in issues being subjected to very different interpretations. For example, when considering whether people with learning disabilities should become parents and should be allowed to keep their children rather than have them placed for adoption, the following views were expressed:

> That detailed IQ testing will provide firm evidence that a mother is competent in the relevant areas to ensure her child's safety. (from a clinical psychologist)

> That, after horrific cases of child deaths and gross neglect, it is essential to be extra-vigilant and avoid any risk of potential scandal and blame of social services. (from a senior social worker)

> That he was pleased to be told of positive examples as he felt we all have the right to parent. (from a man with learning disabilities)

In a forum such as this, professionals have to listen to those voices they may not always pause to hear. Other ways of seeing are confronted. It is a merging of disparate discourses to aid re-thinking or, alternatively, to reinforce ingrained prejudices.

At the heart of these many languages, using their own jargon and work-related texts, is a struggle for universal values. For, if the deconstruction of existing hierarchies is to result in a more liberating and open level of debate, there needs to be a working together to find new ways of saying things which are sensitive to difference; which value those who need help to express their views; and, which does not recreate a new hierarchy every bit as constricting as the old.

Text 3

This Strong Beam of Light

Pride became the password for both deaf and gay people in the 1970s. Deaf gay people's pride grew more and more open in public with both ASL and homosexual desire coming out more and more from the closets of shame. They discovered that the straight deaf community was not too fond of them, so they formed their own chapters of Rainbow Alliance of the Deaf (RAD); the RAD chapters also helped start the tradition of hosting a national convention every other year.

Technology soon made deaf people less dependent on hearing people when using the telephone: TDDs (Telecommunication Devices for the Deaf) got smaller and easier to use. And the deaf community quickly coined abbreviations to help cut down on the cumbersome typing on the keyboard: GA means 'Go Ahead,' SK means 'Stop Keying,' QQ means?, and SMILE means just that.

And every day close captioned television programmes, videotapes and laserdiscs became more common. Deafness is not a handicap, but limited information accessibility is. Most deaf people are looking forward to the day when videophones are affordable and clear enough to catch their signs. Too many deaf people are embarrassed by their 'broken' English.

In the 1980s, AIDS struck. The number of that first generation of openly deaf gay men shrank horribly, and in some cities, local RAD chapters folded. Misinformation and miseducation was the norm with AIDS organizations in their relationships with deaf people.

All this has been a voyage of self-empowerment. To empower ourselves further as deaf lesbians and gay men, we must question everything including whatever our own government, doctors, teachers and parents tell us. If they don't bother to question enough on their own, we are immediately at risk. What they believe to be truths may turn out to be distortions or even lies. And if we don't question them, we may be hurt by their erroneous truths.

For example, consider the controversy raging over cochlea implants. Because the right education at the right time is so crucial to a deaf child's language development, it would have made sense for the deaf community to be consulted prior to such momentous decisions as the federal Food and Drug Administration's appalling approval of cochlea implants on babies two years or older — even though the procedure is obviously far more permanent than hearing aids. (The fact that the FDA did not wait out the required minimum ten-year period of evaluation is even more shocking: They made this decision in a little less than two years.)

At least a deaf person can choose to take hearing aids out and be really deaf in the cultural sense, or put them back in to interact with the hearing world. But cochlea implants mutilate the human head with under 25 percent significant improvement in hearing. That right to choose to be culturally deaf has been summarily removed by parents overwhelmed by doctors and 'experts'. And in their confusion, parents often don't even think of asking to talk with members of the deaf community for a second opinion. Studies conducted on speech perception among children with cochlea implants and among profoundly deaf hearing-aid users show that implanted children hear much less than even profoundly deaf children with hearing aids.

What's more, a cochlea implant operation costs at least $40,000. A pair of hearing aids — if a pair is needed — costs approximately $1,500. The maintenance of the implant — including visits to the doctor and the audiology clinic for extensive speech and hearing therapy — is far more expensive than sending your broken hearing aids out for repair, as well as being far more intrusive in the life of the deaf child. Moreover, the cochlea implantee is stuck with this permanent thing, leading from inside the skull to behind the ear, even though the device could become outdated in a few years. Also, as children's skulls develop, further surgery is required for implant adjustment. The tragedy is that more than 5,000 people, including over 1,000 children, have taken this route. If they're not that rich, guess who's paying? Like many other deaf taxpayers, I don't want my money to support such a questionable enterprise.

And so for us deaf gay people, three big words found their way into our vocabulary. **Paternalism** is the attitude of hearing people who feel compelled to take care of deaf people because the poor things don't know what's best for them. **Homophobia** is the fear and hatred of gay people, and **audism** is the attitude of hearing people who make themselves authorities on deafness but do not allow deaf people to be equals in decision-making processes in deaf affairs, including deaf education. With awareness of these three concepts and their implications, we are that much more capable of greater self-empowerment. (from Luczak, R. (ed.) (1993) *Eyes of Desire*)

Questions

1 What do you think the author means by the phrase 'a voyage of self-empowerment'? Is the travelling metaphor apt?
2 Here is a clear example of conflict between medical discourses and deaf culture. How do you respond to the concept of 'that right to choose to be culturally deaf': does it shock you?
3 The 'three big words' in the vocabulary of deaf gay people reflect my assertion in the introduction to this book; that 'special needs' language emerges from sentimentality, arrogance and hate. Why is it important for deaf gay people to recognize the implications of these words?

4   Struggling with Political Correctness

Introduction

When the special language, which is no longer useful to us, is deconstructed and changed, who will decide what is going to take its place? Language is a source of power and control and, as such, to be contested: words need to be won. The battle for political correctness is between those who feel comfortable with certain words and those who express unease. The voice of enlightened modernity promotes a liberalism which indicates that concessions are made and old usage refined. Yet this is insufficient for many political activists who feel that this is an establishment language, powerful and authoritative, and with an arrogance which denies differences of perception and intuition.

In this chapter, I shall explore elements of this struggle with political correctness. It has been a topic of increasing popularity among social science academics and, for the purposes of discussion, I shall draw particularly upon ideas within recent papers written by an American sociologist (Zola, 1993) and by myself, reflecting a specifically British context (Corbett, 1994a). I feel that making connections between British and American theorists is valuable as it helps to clarify what unites us and where we differ in contexts and experiences.

This chapter will be presented in two distinct halves. The first half is a reflective analysis of the traditional use of language relating to disability; the second half is an exploration of the struggle for a political correctness in the way words are employed. This division is an indicator of the tensions inherent in special education provision and practice, wherein professional authority has long dominated and effectively silenced the voices of those who are labelled and categorized. The struggle with political correctness is both a personal fight and a collective battle to create new territories.

The Power of Naming

In this first section, I shall discuss the following: the use of aggressive metaphors in relation to special education; the definition of 'special'; the effect of restrictive categories on treatment and perceptions; and, the struggle between physical realities and metaphorical terms. To set the scene for this debate, I shall explore the power of naming in relation to perceptions of special need.

Zola observed that the tenacity of a name meant that 'any unnaming process is not without its difficulties and consequences' (1993, p. 167). Names confer status and identity. Even the letters attached to names contribute further to this identification. Thus OBE is a mark of distinction, whilst ESN is a source of stigma. It is not a purely frivolous comparison. Both the naming of an 'Order of the British Empire' (OBE) and a status of 'Educationally Sub-Normal' (ESN) are judgments. These are made by people, within specific cultures at a particular time in history. Selection for honorary awards is dependent upon what that culture perceives as noteworthy at that period — acts of distinction are measured differently as decades change. Similarly, measurements of educational deficiency change. The power of naming is such that the labels and letters remain as an influence on social standing and self-perception long after their initial judgments were made and have been subsequently modified, overturned or rendered null and void.

Perhaps a particularly useful example of the power of naming in relation to special education was seen in the person of Sir Cyril Burt. In this individual, there was both a recipient of the naming which conveys distinction, and the power to name others as 'backward' through newly designed processes. He might be viewed as the 'father' of naming, legitimating a commitment to confer high status upon the discipline of educational psychology and upon the process of naming degrees of difficulty. Yet the use of data in elements of his research has been challenged, discredited and, in the process, threatened the status which was given to his name.

In Chapter 2, I explained the ways in which the language of psychology, sociology and philosophy gradually usurped the dominance of medicine in special education. If we examine the way in which texts of the mid-1970s perceived key issues in special education, it is clear that Burt's influence was to act as a bridge between the power of the medical establishment in naming special needs and the new-found power of naming which constituted educational psychology. In a collection of *Orientations in Special Education*, edited by Klaus Wedell, who has become one of the central figures in the field of special needs in the

1980s and 1990s, the struggle to categorize was shown to be of particular concern:

> Strangely, despite the pioneering work of Burt (1925, 1937), the epidemiological approach has rarely been applied in the area of educational disorders, at least not until recently. In part, this is probably because of the greater difficulty in defining what constitutes an educational disorder as opposed to a medical disorder. This difficulty in agreement over definition occurs despite the availability of standardized attainment tests. When it comes to deciding whether a child is showing a behavioral or emotional difficulty, the problems are even greater. And yet one must agree on definitions in all these areas before one can begin to count the numbers of children falling into each category of disorder. (Yule, 1975, p. 18)

In this text of twenty years ago there is an indication of why Warnock's (1978) unnaming process of applying the generic term 'special educational needs' has continued to be problematic since its inception. Just as these professionals were struggling both to establish and consolidate the status of their naming, i.e., as educational psychologists, and to delineate clear categories of names, they were being threatened with a move to 'unname'. It is no surprise, if we acknowledge this scenario, that the naming of 'special educational needs' became subverted into a form which suited those who feared the loss of their power to name.

Attacking the Problem

As I noted in my investigations of the use of language in special education texts (Corbett, 1994a), it has been a common feature of using metaphorical concepts that anything associated with disability is given negative connotations. Thus, authors refer to the 'attack' on illiteracy in the same way that doctors speak of attacking the sources of disease. Whilst there is an evident logic in this thinking, if disease and disability are always equated with danger, it is an oppressive use of language when applied to people rather than to specific diseases.

If an aggressive approach is fostered in the use of 'attacking' metaphors, this can surely lead to an oppressive experience for the recipients of this verbal assault. To return to my own teaching life, working in special schools in the 1970s and early 1980s, the individual programmes designed to modify specific behaviours in pupils could be seen to oppress in their intensity. It is as though, when attacking a disabling condition which is perceived as detrimental to a full learning experience, the sensitivity to individual differences can be ignored. I have seen teachers encouraged to 'attack' a behaviour in a child, as if this exists in isolation, with the individual as an appendage. For 'special' children, the sense of self can become distorted and denied if a disproportionate emphasis is put upon elements of behaviour, deficiency and limitations.

Defining 'Special'

There are certain words in our language which have meanings so obtuse as to slip from our grasp as we reach for them. I feel this about 'special'. It is a word that fills me with unease. Whilst it has the meaning within it to convey that which is positive, I rarely feel comfortable with the way it is generally applied. If 'special' is so positive, why is it not usurped by the patriarchy and widely employed to define power and status? Theweleit (1994), a German philosopher, suggests that it is the supreme confidence and self-love of the male ego which makes men place women on pedestals as 'special'. If they are seen as 'better' this renders them powerless but nice. As Theweleit implies, women today resist being idealized and then used for some end, declaring themselves to be simply *different* but not *better*. How can this version of 'special' be viewed as a desirable state if it accompanies an acknowledgment of social and personal weakness? We relish difference. We reject being 'special'.

I would like to apply Thewelweit's analysis to people with disabilities and learning difficulties, or those with physical or learning disabilities or, as they often now prefer to be called, disabled people. Whatever terminology is used, there is an analogy between the powerless status of women and that of disabled people. When the term 'special' is applied to disabled people, it emphasizes their relative powerlessness rather than conferring them with honour and dignity. As I pointed out earlier in this Chapter (The Power of Naming, pp. 47–48) the term ESN (educationally sub-normal) defines a markedly contrasting form of 'special' to the term OBE (Order of the British Empire). Yet both are signs of distinction. Those who put OBE after their names do so with pride. No person would wish to attach ESN — or whatever the current label, e.g., SLD (severe learning disabilities) to their name. It marks them as 'special' but not better. It is a negative naming rendered harmless by an implication of 'niceness'.

If we are struggling with the term 'special', we need to assess how people with learning disabilities have been treated by being seen as 'better', in the sense of lacking the ruthlessness and selfishness which are seen as human (male) traits. They have been traditionally portrayed as simple innocents, unable to protect themselves, requiring supervision and care and incapable of coping with adult relationships or decision making. This leaves them in a permanent child-like state, in which their morality remains stainless in a direct relationship with their personal and social powerlessness. There is a high price to pay for this 'niceness'. It is not desirable to remain in a child-like state. Innocence is retained at the cost of experience; niceness keeps people harmless and passive. Professionals and carers have a significant investment in keeping 'special' as a concept of niceness. If people with learning disabilities are seen as 'different' but not 'better', they no longer count as 'special', therefore, they should be entitled to the same rights and expectations as the rest of the adult population. They can also be seen as other than nice.

Alongside my personal discomfort with the word 'special', is an innate resistance to the concept of 'nice' when applied to disabled people. It is a reflection of the way in which they are socially marginalized and seen as 'other'. Like the placing on a pedestal of women for being 'better' (and therefore, less liable to challenge or resist), it marks them as incapable of the range of human characteristics that constitute social interaction. There are some kind, gentle, good-humoured disabled people. There are some ill-natured, aggressive, devious disabled people. Some are deeply prejudiced against other minorities. Others are open-minded and receptive to change. In other words, disabled people are like the rest of the human population in being diverse, complex and vulnerable. If we portray them as 'special' and, by implication, 'better' we deny them their humanity.

This attachment to niceness persists, particularly in the charity business where disabled people are neatly packaged and sold to the public. In a recent investigation of the approach that a large British charity for people with learning disabilities is adopting, the promotion of niceness was clearly evident (Corbett and Ralph, 1994). All the visual images were happy and uplifting (literally, in that raised arms were extensively visible). Do we have to continue to promote disabled people as 'better', in their permanent 'sunny' dispositions, because if we show them as merely human they lose their 'special' qualities? It seems important to me to stop equating 'special' with 'better' but to see it as demonstrating difference, a difference that can be respected, acknowledged and seen as an active agent for change, rather than a passive recipient of services.

Boxing People In

The mania for categorizing 'special needs' into neat and distinctive sections is to be found in educational texts of the 1970s. There was a particular fondness for the careful distinguishing between ESN(M) and ESN(S). In this process the (S), which denoted 'severe', was seen to require a distinctly different treatment from the (M), which was only 'moderate'. If some pupils had 'severe' learning difficulties or, in the terms of those times, were 'severely sub-normal', they had to be given a more carefully structured programme in relation to their perceived needs. The criteria by which children were judged to be (S) or (M) were culture and context related. In an article of that period, Tizard (1966) refers to 'handicapped' children in remedial provision — a term that would later only be applied to those whose difficulties were perceived as 'severe'.

Booth, in a reflection which was both self-deprecatory and critical of professional practice, noted that:

> in my colleagues' encounters with pupils they did not seem to notice that there was a stigma associated with special schooling, particularly those designated ESN(M), which parents tried to resist. (1988, p. 115)

If 'special' was a benign term linked with privileged attention and care, why did parents and perceptive educational psychologists recognize its danger. Once designated 'special', a process of treatment which excluded and confined was reified as 'structured'. The god of Structure ruled special education during the early 1980s, until we began to question its omnipotence.

Ainscow and Tweddle were to promote a structured learning approach which was to have a profound effect on teachers. When we were told,

> The teacher who has developed the art of presenting work at an appropriate pace, minimizing the likelihood of prolonged exposure to failure and ensuring success at each stage in the learning of a new skill, has developed *skills of task analysis.* (Ainscow and Tweddle, 1979, p. 25, my emphasis)

what were we to do other than attempt to develop these skills as fast as possible? In the special school in which I worked at that time, teachers (and young, enthusiastic and newly qualified teachers particularly) were desperate for structure. Special education in the early 1970s had been characterized by casual methods, dependent upon charismatic individuals and *ad hoc* approaches. Here, now, was a box for us to fit our pupils into: tidy, measurable, recordable, detailed and tightly monitored. It was secure and made us feel professionally competent.

Some years later, Ainscow (1989) was to reflect that he came to regret those boxes of individual tasks analysis, for they led to an impoverished social experience for the learners and a loss of flexibility in the teachers. I always encourage my students at the University of East London to be aware of how writers can and do change their minds. It is a real danger to quote an author in a 1980 statement without also investigating their subsequent development and reflections. Both Booth and Ainscow are examples of well-known authors in the field of British special education who have modified their views within a series of reflections. This process demonstrates the way in which we all struggle with our changing perceptions and reconsider our use of language, our way of perceiving appropriate provision and our recognition of contextual factors.

Physical Realities and Metaphorical Terms

One of the struggles that disabled activists are continuing to contend with, both in Britain and America, is the extent to which physical realities can and should be ignored in the emphasis on metaphorical terms. Whilst a battle for semantics is important on one level, there are the other daily struggles over pain, discomfort and frustration. Zola, in his evaluation of the American context, suggested that,

> We must seek a change in the connotations and the pervasiveness of our names without denying the essential reality of our conditions. (1993, p. 170)

In the British disability movement, Morris (1991) was one of the key articulators of the 'personal as political' in disability politics with an emphasis upon relating individual experience to collective consciousness. She demonstrated that the metaphors needed to grow from the personal struggle, not deny it.

Where metaphorical terms are so significant is in their use of positive, proud and forceful imagery. Disability has for so long been equated with personal tragedy, misery, suffering and weakness. As Morris explains,

We object to words like suffer, condemned, confined, victim,
and to negative images portraying disability. (1991, p. 110)

Instead of presenting the wheelchair image as a symbol of imprison-
ment, she suggests that disabled people see it as a means of mobility,
movement, freedom and independence. The symbol itself is a restricted
metaphor indicating that disability always equates with physical restric-
tions, whereas it encompasses a diverse range of experiences.

In order to incorporate their experiences of physical reality, disabled people are seeking new metaphors, images which are positive,
active, dynamic and even humorous. Cartoonists, like the American
Callahan, provide a range of provocative images of disability — definitely not 'PC' in their bold irreverence.

This exploration of bad taste in disability imagery could be seen as
the antidote to tragic imagery, mocking and teasing instead of display-
ing misery.

Defensive Subcultures

In the second half of this chapter, I intend to lead in to those issues
which will be explained in detail in the next chapter, 'Listening to New
Voices'. These new voices have emerged from the struggle with political correctness and are born of the disability movement. What distinguishes them from the voice of enlightened modernity and the
establishment of medicine, educational psychology and the academy, is
that they are mouthed by those with direct and personal experience of
disability.

In this section, the following areas will be introduced to be developed further in 'Listening to New Voices': shaping defensive subcultures;
renegotiating naming; making active; cohesiveness and clarity.

It is the nature of defensive subcultures that they resist external
definitions and create their own metaphors. Zola suggested that the
issue of naming, therefore, becomes one of the first battle grounds for
minority groups. He reflected that both fostering a collective pride and
creating a defensive subculture was made more difficult for disabled
people by the nature of their isolation and diversity of experience.

In a recent paper (Corbett, 1994b) I have explored the relationship
between disability politics and gay pride. In a sense the disability
movement can be seen to have gained strength, support and momentum from the black civil rights movement, women's liberation and gay
pride. All demonstrate the power of defensive subcultures to redefine

"Don't worry, he won't get far on foot."

John Callahan, 1992 (postcard produced by Statics)

the language, create new metaphors and reshape imagery from negative to positive.

Renegotiating Naming

Zola expressed caution at the capacity for the disability subculture to create a proud naming, to associate themselves with other minority groups:

> With the rise of black power, a derogatory label became a rallying cry, 'Black is Beautiful' and when women saw their strength in numbers, they shouted 'Sisterhood is Powerful'. But what about those with a chronic illness or disability? Could they yell, 'Long Live Cancer', 'Up with Multiple Sclerosis', 'I'm glad I had Polio!', 'Don't you wish you were Blind?' Thus the traditional reversing of the stigma will not so easily provide a basis for a common positive identity. (1993, p. 168)

I think that this scepticism highlights the tensions between physical realities and metaphorical terms. Disabled people are not denying the pain and discomfort they experience when they express pride and dignity in their lives. In a recent reflection on her accident which led to disability, Morris recognizes that,

> My physical impairment is not something I would choose. I would rather be able to walk than have to use a wheelchair. I would rather the spasm in my legs didn't wake me up at six o'clock in the morning. I would rather I didn't have to worry about incontinence when I share a bed with someone. I would rather I didn't have the burning sensation in my legs which is there every waking moment of my day and night. Yet I love how I am and the life I lead. I like what I see when I look in the mirror. I value so much the contact I have with other disabled people — and with non-disabled allies — in our struggle against prejudice and discrimination. (1994, pp. 170–1).

In this frank account, she demonstrates that disability pride can co-exist with an acknowledgment of physical realities. The difficulties do not negate the pride.

When I drew parallels between the language of gay pride and disability politics, I was particularly concerned with the way in which we have been able to renegotiate negative labelling to create our own positive labels. The labels of stigma, embodied in Goffman's (1968) analysis, present us as abnormal, deviant, weak, and on the margins of society. If disabled people read the recent best-selling political mouthings in Alan Clark's (1994) *Diaries*, they will discover that this influential minister, when in the Department of Employment, was irritated to be presented to a group of disabled people as he wanted to meet only those who could really be seen as employable. So stigma flourishes in Whitehall. For those of us who are gay or lesbian, we have confirmation in the British national press of August 1994 that our contributions, however competent, are not required in the armed forces, royal airforce or navy. We are perceived as unsuitable. If those of us who feel pushed to the margins simply for being ourselves are not able to renegotiate our own labels, we run a real danger of submitting to the damaging stigmas and seeing only the difficulties in our difference.

Disability pride is about self-respect, just as black pride and gay pride are ways of celebrating diversity. As Morris (1994) says in the previous extract, a great source of joy, comfort and support comes from solidarity with those who share a commitment to change. On our own, we lack the power to redefine language and disseminate new images. Collectively, we have strength and vigour.

Making Active

One of the traditional interpretations of disability is that it relates to passivity, dependency, neediness and pathos. It is not surprising, therefore, that the voices of disabled people have not been heard in the dominant discourses. It is unusual for people with physical or learning disabilities to gain professional status, political power or to be evident in the media. For many years, the voices which reflect the experiences of disabled people's lives have been effectively muted.

Within academic life, recent efforts have been made to include these voices. In Britain, this took the form of a series of disability seminars, in which disabled academics and political activists shared their perceptions with non-disabled peers ('Disability, Handicap and Society', 1992). In America, Shapiro (1993) has collated the history of the Disability Civil Rights Movements in the USA, to demonstrate the extent of its influence on current legislation and attitudes.

What has become evident in recent years is that the disability movement internationally has grown and strengthened. It is angry and forcefully vociferous. The passivity has been replaced by action. Whilst those disabled people who chose to be politically active represent only a proportion of the disabled population, they are bringing in new voices to the debate on terminology, images and power.

Cohesiveness and Clarity

I shall conclude this chapter by summarizing what I see as the key issues in the struggle for political correctness and the main features to emerge from this struggle. The first step is to recognize the power of naming. This is a formal structure, imposed through establishment values and rarely challenged. The next aspect in this struggle is to reject the term 'special' as demeaning and confining, conferring a child-like status on those who wish to claim their adulthood. A recognition of physical reality is essential. Without it, we are denying what makes us human. What needs to be challenged is the language which retains a metaphorical suffering, pathos and dependency. Through collective political strength, new positive metaphors will emerge to celebrate difference and demonstrate pride and self-respect.

The main features of disability pride have emerged in cohesiveness and clarity. In coming together to share support and gain political power, disabled people have renegotiated the language. Their collective energy has rejuvenated imagery. Humour, zest for living, and healthy aggression have at last destroyed the passive stereotype and displayed the multifaceted features of disability. What is being sought now is clarity of expression. Language is carefully considered. Words are weighed up. Those in the disability movement reject the 'pussy-footing' around that many non-disabled people engage in as they flounder with embarrassment to avoid offence. Words need to be clear unambiguous and powerful. They need to spike and make a direct impact on the listener. Disabled people are recognizing this and employing a language which is immediate, shocking, provocative and saying,

'Look at Me. I am as I am and pleased to be so. Take me or leave me but don't ignore and don't patronize.'

Text 4

No Pity

One of the most common attacks on the disability movement is to mock the politically correct terms often used to describe disability. Yet it is almost always non-disabled people — relying on the stereotype that a disabled person should be an inspiration overcoming some challenge — who use prettifying euphemisms. Virtually no disabled person uses these cute phrases. Concoctions like 'the vertically challenged' are silly and scoffed at. The 'differently abled', the 'handi-capable', or the 'physically and mentally challenged' are almost universally dismissed as too gimmicky and too inclusive. 'Physically challenged doesn't distinguish me from a woman climbing Mt Everest, something certainly I'll never do,' says Nancy Mairs, an essayist and poet with multiple sclerosis. 'It blurs the distinction between our lives.' Only by using direct terminology, she argues, will people think about what it means to be disabled and the accommodations she needs, such as wheelchair-accessible buildings or grab bars in bathrooms.

Dianne Piastro, who writes the syndicated column 'Living with a disability', complains that such terms suggest that disability is somehow shameful and needs to be concealed in a vague generality. 'It's denying our reality instead of saying that our reality, of being disabled, is okay,' says Piastro. Mary Johnson, editor of *The Disability Rag*, complains that such euphemistic terms come from nondisabled 'do-gooders' who 'wouldn't understand disability culture if we ran over their toes with a wheelchair'. These words have 'no soul' and 'no power', says Johnson. 'They're like vanilla custard.'

Is there a word with the requisite soul power? There was a surprise when Johnson's magazine surveyed its readers. Newly in vogue among some physically disabled people is the very word that is the ultimate in offensiveness to others: 'cripple'. 'It's like a raised gnarled fist,' says Cheryl Wade, a Berkeley, California, performance artist, who likes 'crippled' because it is a blunt and accurate description of her body, which has been twisted by rheumatoid arthritis. 'Crips', 'gimps', and 'blinks' have long been for the exclusive, internal use by people of those disabilities. (Terms for nondisabled people include 'walkies' and 'a.b.s' for able-bodied and 'TABs' for the 'temporarily able-bodied', a you'll-get-yours-yet reminder that disability hits most of us in old age if not before.)

'Cripple' will not become safe for general usage right away, but its newfound popularity shows that the stigma of disability is being rejected and replaced with a pride in being identified as disabled. Mairs, another who prefers 'cripple', compares the change to the civil rights movement's replacement of 'Negro' with 'black'. In reclaiming 'cripple', disabled people are taking the thing in their identity that scares the outside world the most and making it a cause to revel in with militant self-pride. That disabled people are re-appropriating words to redefine themselves and thinking about 'the power of negative language', says Brandeis University sociology professor Irving Kenneth Zola, is a sign of a new and thriving group identity. (from Shapiro, J. (1993) *No Pity*, New York, Times Books, pp. 33–4)

Questions

1 Why do we use politically correct terms? What are the dangers of becoming obsessed with avoiding oppressive or distasteful language? Reflect on some of the words in the past used to describe disabilities. Why have we changed them? What makes our new words better?

2 How do you interpret the term 'Soul Partner', as used in the text? What degree of empathy is implied?

3 Why do you think that 'the power of negative language' is a sign of a strong group identity? Can you compare disability politics to black pride and gay pride? Taking words like 'cripple' and 'queer', how can they be made into symbols of pride rather than stigma?

5   Listening to New Voices

Introduction

In the struggle for political correctness, new voices have emerged to influence the disability discourse. These are no longer the voices of the medical establishment: neither are they those of enlightened modernity. They are the voices of disabled theorists, forging new ways of thinking built on direct experience. New voices are also heard from the disability movement, offering political dogma and the clarity born of frustration and anger.

In order to set these voices into the context that awaited them, I shall begin this chapter with a reflection upon the impact of earlier discourses. These will be divided into the voice of enlightened modernity and voices whose emphasis brought different dimensions to the debate. The central section of this chapter will explore the voices of disabled academics, the celebration of difference in diverse voices and the metaphorical shift to anger rather than passivity.

Hearing Enlightened Modernity

If we are to recognize the extent to which this voice influenced thinking, we need to listen again to Mary Warnock, whose official inquiries over the last twenty years have included the environment, educating children with special needs, animal experiments, teachers and, most controversially, embryology. She is called upon, by governments, to bring her perceptions as a moral philosopher into a wide range of debates.

When she reflected on the Warnock Committee of Inquiry, she made the statement, quoted in Text I, that,

> education was a track along which *EVERY* child and adult has
> a right to walk, *a right of way.* (Warnock, 1991, p. 147)

This statement, simple in its directness, conveys a level of certainty that has to be challenged. In Chapter One, I suggested that there was an indication that one approach only should be appropriate for conceptualizing 'need'. If we are to include new voices, we must also question what Warnock means by her reference to enabling 'children as far as possible to progress along this track' (*ibid.*). I would rather conclude that education, certainly as it exists in Britain and America, is not 'a track' but a vast *series of tracks* that will lead to very different destinations.

Warnock displays the naivety and complacency of establishment values when offering personal perspectives in interviews. In a recent example of national British journalism (the *Observer* magazine, *Life*, 24th July 1994), she admitted to the interviewer that it was most important to her that her children went to Oxbridge and that her family came out top. She suggests that she accepts being called one of the 'great and the good' and displays her elitism in the reflection that philosophers like herself are the best people for royal commissions and committees of inquiry, as,

> If you are running a sweetie shop you are actually going to lose money if you spend too much time on a committee. (Warnock, 1978, quoted by Billen, 1994, in the *Observer Magazine*, p. 10)

Her sentiments are redolent of those nineteenth-century aristocrats protesting about the vulgarity of those in 'trade'. It is as if a legacy of class discourse persists and permeates conceptualization. It perpetuates an out-dated divisive and excluding approach to education. This 'track' (top public school — Oxbridge — the elite professions) is one we might all have 'a right to walk' but this kind of right counts for nothing. The dangers in listening only to this voice are that the embodiment of where the right track leads is found in members of the British Parliament Tory Establishment. This is vividly illustrated in Alan Clark's *Diaries*, which are littered with references to his days at Eton and Oxford. He acknowledges that his behaviour towards women is outrageous.

> (I fear that if I'd come from 'an underprivileged background' I'd probably by now have done time for GBH, or assault, or even what nanny calls *The other*.) (1994, p. 229)

In addition to his particular educational track, the reference throughout to 'nanny' marks the other distinguishing features of a privileged (but hardly typical) experience. His favourite expression of disfavour is 'totally spastic' — no attempt at political correctness there. The advantages which his educational track gave him are evident: no matter how antisocial his behaviour, his class will bail him out.

There is a patent dishonesty in the inference that we share the same educational track. Where would our marked social differences, based more on class in Britain and on wealth in America, be demonstrated were it not for the wide variety of tracks? To select the track used by the establishment to educate its children requires resources unavailable to most. For others, their tracks are severely limited and enforced rather than chosen. Recognizing this reality, how can we listen, with anything other than incredulity, to phrases like 'a right to walk'?

Voices from the Academy

In Chapter 2, I explained the different tracks and boundaries that compose the 'special needs' discourses. These voices have influenced imagery and attitudes, each with their specific emphasis. They also reflect spaces of confrontation and conflict. An interesting example of this occurrence illustrates how the new voices of disabled theorists are challenging and criticizing the non-disabled voices in the Academy. There was a long-running dialogue in the *European Journal of Special Education* between Soder, Booth and Oliver (Soder, 1989, 1991; Booth, 1991; Oliver, 1992b). The two non-disabled writers were arguing over the way in which 'integration' should be defined and perceived. Oliver who has been disabled since his late teens, offered a response which was both angry and impatient. He taunted them with the accusation that their quibble about the intricacies of semantics amounted to little more than the indulgence of 'mutual masturbation'.

This challenge to the words used by non-disabled theorists is redolent of the arguments relating to imagery presented in Chapter 4. The disabled political activists are impatient with the preciousness and overt hypersensitivity of non-disabled academics, seeking to find the least offensive vocabulary in the minefield of good taste. Speaking the 'right' language is *not* about agonizing over delicate sensibilities. It is courageous, clear and strong. That is why Oliver provokes with 'mutual masturbation'. He is saying to those who fear giving offence — 'Get on with it. Stop playing around and *act.*' (my emphasis — not his actual words but my interpretation)

One of the ways in which the Academy itself is being changed is in the increased inclusion of disabled theorists. Whilst few disabled people become academics — a reflection of the destructive effects of special education and low expectations — their numbers are rising and new voices are now heard. This is gradually altering the tone and imagery of the discourse and shifting the boundaries in the process.

Voices of Disabled Theorists and Echoes in the Academy

Two of the key disabled theorists in Britain who have succeeded in developing new discourses are Finkelstein (e.g., 1980, 1993) and Oliver (e.g., 1990, 1992). Both have fostered disability studies as a legitimate area in the Academy. The discourse that they have created and sustained is that of the social model of disability. This is a discourse that demonstrates the ways in which social, economic and cultural factors determine experiences of disability, rather than all problems arising from personal difficulties. It has had a profound influence on the language of 'special needs'.

Oliver, in his sociological approach to disability, has both conceptualized 'special need' as a social and political construct related to a context in culture and history and has established the academic status of examining attitudes to disability. Finkelstein, in his forceful imagery, has presented visual representations of a world in which being non-disabled is a disadvantage and has shown that solidarity and collective anger can forge new ways of viewing an area of study. As these two disabled academics have gained prominence in their field they may be said to have created their own form of enlightened modernity. They are powerful figures in disability studies, whose theories are widely explored and evaluated. In the process of breaking into the academic establishment and fostering a new area of scholarship, they have inevitably grown into part of that hierarchy, becoming figures who hold themselves up for judgment. Now that they have established this respectable base from which to build, they have opened up a discourse that allows for dissent and argument over language, imagery and the focus of development.

In order to illustrate the broad elements of a social model of disability that have permeated the use of language and imagery, I shall take two American examples and two British. I want to explore specifically focused texts and those that relate to general educational issues. It is important to set 'special needs' into a wider context which addresses aspects of major concern common to all learners. Unless we do this, we are colluding with a segregated area of language use, designed to apply to certain individuals rather than to us all. My focus will be on two elements of disability language use: the creation of imagery; and the development of discourses.

Chappell, a British researcher, refers to Wolfensberger, the extremely influential American academic, as a proponent of 'authoritarian conservatism' (1992, p. 43). His emphasis within the normalization debate has been on avoiding the stigma of deviancy and acquiring socially valued roles. Chappell, in her analysis, indicates that making people with learning disabilities appear more normal avoids presenting an unconditional acceptance. The imagery created by her critique of the normalization principle is one of enlightened modernity and a vision of the 'right track' (i.e., the establishment route). This time, however, it is an American rather than a British model, representing the academic establishment rather than the class hierarchy. Wolfensberger's influence on the normalization debate has been extensive and it has been based on the premise that there is a 'normal' track to pursue and guide deviant individuals towards, if they are to enjoy the status of valued social roles. If we listen to new voices in the disability movement we can hear the diversity of experience and preference — the wealth of potential 'routes' to a rich social life in the range of sub-stratas of society.

Walford explores the effect of a market concept on schooling. He suggests that 'choosing a school for a child is not directly analogous to buying a packet of cornflakes' as 'children are different from cornflakes' (1994, p. 5). His imagery conjures up a picture of treating people like products, to be standardized, packaged and promoted to a buying public. 'Special needs' fit neatly into such an analogy by constitution: those cornflakes which are too burnt, misshapen or irregular to be included can be sold as a cut-price economy version. Ball, in exploring the discourse of policy, notes that,

> Discourses are about what can be said, and thought, but also about who can speak, when, where and with what authority. Discourses embody the meaning and use of propositions and words. (1994, p. 21)

In his analysis of the discourse of policy, heavily influenced by Foucault (1977), Ball demonstrates that languages and metaphors evolve out of the mixture of voices allowed the space to be heard.

Ball and Walford reflect the British context in which the experiences of schooling for all is now driven by a market culture but where the discourse of policy is ripe for deconstruction and a realignment of power as new voices emerge to challenge and provoke. Gerber, reflecting the American picture suggests that,

> So powerful is the voice of disabled people becoming, and so powerful are the intellectual and ideological forces that seek to give that voice centrality in shaping the discussion of disability, that it may soon become difficult to recall that a short time ago

people with disabilities were little more than the *objects* of study.
(1990, p. 4)

If we apply Ball's approach to policy and Walford's recognition of
market forces, it is apparent that the language of special needs has
entered a new arena. Changes have occurred that have made a tangible
difference. Among the new developments are the following: the formation of a disability enlightened modernity to create an establishment
to challenge; the placing of the special needs discourse in the context
of the market place by Warnock (1991) and others; the inclusion of
divergent voices in the special needs discourse, to counteract conservative concepts of 'normality' and to postulate new ways of seeing
differences.

Celebrating Difference

There are many different voices now emerging which reflect the diversity in society. They may be heard from disabled feminists, black disabled people, those who are gay and disabled. In these voices we can
hear a multiplicity of experience and expression.

One of the most valuable contributions of new voices is their sharing
of actual feelings, day-to-day living, and experience of professional
care. Just as the special education theorists need to be matched with
corresponding examples of daily practice and classroom experience, so
the social model of disability needs to be applied to the daily living
experience. Baily (1994) offers a valuable insight, for example, into her
feelings of being treated as a disabled body, not a person, when in
residential care:

> They identified residents by our intimate physical needs, judged
> us by how we said we wanted those needs to be met. I felt
> myself diminish beneath the weight of others judging, defining;
> I felt my self shrink in the shrinking space. (1994, p. 35)

This reflection indicates that, in the case of individual experience rather
than academic theory, the medical model of care is perpetuated. Cross
(1994) supports this inference, with her suggestion that paid carers
often tend to see disabled children as disembodied disabilities,

> Called by their equipment ('He's a catheter'), their conditions
> ('she's a CP'), or procedures necessary in their care ('she's a

toileter') — in fact almost anything except their names. (1994, p. 165)

One of the implications of listening to these voices, speaking from direct and immediate experience, is that those who take responsibilities for the daily care of disabled people are often unfamiliar with or even perhaps hostile to, the social theory of disability. Just as the gap between aspects of special education theory and practice are clearly evident, so the disabled theorists are often ignored in the behaviour towards disabled people in everyday settings.

Rieser suggests that whilst many teachers will challenge language which discriminates against various social groups, they often fail to apply this to the 'special needs' area:

In order to move from the 'form' to the 'content' of integration from a static to a dynamic and ongoing view, in short from integration to inclusion; teachers, school workers, governors and parents need to re-assess their own thinking, language and attitudes about special needs and disability. (1994, p. 11)

He goes on to illustrate the kind of vocabulary that fails to celebrate difference but which rather perpetuates negative labelling and promotes a low self-image:

bright — stupid
able — dull/not able
smart — backward or remedial
clever — thick
intelligent — unintelligent
gifted/talented — useless/untalented
well-adjusted — disturbed
fit — handicapped
alert — dopey

Such words tend to be casually used in schools to distinguish degrees of ability. With the increased emphasis on competition and comparison, prompted by a market ethos (Ball, 1994; Walford, 1994), such words are likely to be retained to persist in their negative effect.

Not all teachers are caught in the trap of stereotypical language or imagery based on narrowly defined behavioural techniques. Here is a story told by a teacher that celebrates the different ways in which we all learn:

It was a pupil who finally brought me to question the hypothesis that behavioral psychology represented the last word on the subject of learning. I had been trying to toilet-train Mary for months and was beginning to have some success. Mary liked my guitar playing. It seemed to relax her enough to enable her to let go, as it were. So I had taken to playing Mary a tune as she sat on her potty. We were having some success but the educational psychologist knew that my methods were unorthodox. He undertook to train Mary for me and disappeared into the toilet area with Mary, some charts, a stop watch and a bag of sweets. He persevered for some time but Mary did not approve of this regime. She clearly resented being separated from the group for long periods of time and shut up in the toilet with a stranger, even if he did have a never-ending supply of sweets. Mary with-held her urine and cried. She persevered for quite sometime until the educational psychologist went away with his blank charts, his stop watch and his sweets and Mary was able to rejoin her pals. I got the guitar and again went back to being unorthodox and approximate.

I tell this story in detail because I believe that it is in its small way, profoundly instructive and because I am indebted to Mary, who incidentally became a fully continent music-lover, for its lesson. Mary's toilet-training did not, in the end, depend upon a simple mechanistic view of behaviour. It depended upon social relationships, upon Mary's mood, upon whether she felt happy and relaxed. It was actually a complex phenomenon. It depended upon me taking account of who Mary was as a person. Could I have translated this into behavioral lore? 'Happy' and 'relaxed' are, of course, problematic concepts for behaviourists. How could they be quantified? Place Mary on the potty? Ensure that she is smiling and refraining from biting her nails? I doubt whether this approach would have had any more success than the stop watch and sweets. I came to rely instead upon a degree of intuition and *leavened the dough of my precision teaching* with a healthy measure of humanity, as, of course, did many teachers of children with learning difficulties. (Byers, 1994, pp. 80–81, my emphasis)

I love this story. I feel that it reflects what has long been the experience of many such teachers (I worked in a similar fashion with 'Marys' in the 1970s). It also offers a refreshing example of how we can all adapt and find ways of celebrating the pleasure of difference.

I chose to emphasize the words 'leavened the dough of my precision teaching'. In this image, Byers implies that the art of teaching is creative and we have the ultimate power, however prescriptive the programme, to make the experience our own. To a certain extent, those teachers who remain in special schools need to cultivate skills of subversive creativity if they are to resist the pervading atrophy of a decaying system. In a recent newspaper article (the *Guardian*, September 12 1994) Scott refers to special schools as 'coming to the end of their shelf life' (p. 4) like so many stale buns. It needs characters like Byers to 'leaven the dough', shifting the imagery.

Morris has written extensively of the need to include the personal experiences of disabled people within any political debate. A social model devoid of individuality can be arid. Casling, speaking as a Disability Equality Trainer, said:

> Although the 'social model' has for some time served us well as a way of directing attention away from the personal to the political, I feel now that the debate has been hampered by the rather rigid genealogy of disability thinking. (1993, p. 203)

He prefers to apply a postmodernist approach, using language as the behavioural text and source of metaphor. What Casling found in the workshops he ran, was that the most ostensibly politically correct participants were producing stereotypical images from myths and legends when engaged in group story-telling about disabled characters. Feelings of 'anger', 'guilt' and 'frustration' surfaced. Mythological disabled figures are often pathetic or evil. Our assumptions may be that with the impact of a social model we can no longer see disabled people in this restricted and marginalized way, as if they are other than human.

Yet among what has been termed 'the silent majority' (i.e., those conservative thinkers, with a small and often large 'C', who represent 'middle-of-the-road', reactionary opinions, resistant to change), there is an evident retention of negative imagery relating to disability. In our research, Sue Ralph and I (Corbett and Ralph, 1994) found that the relaunch of the MENCAP new image was slow to be assimilated by the provincial press, reflecting this 'silent majority' conservatism. The public at large, and vested interest groups in particular, would only accept what they felt comfortable with. Too intense a degree of assentation and confidence among disabled people appears to frighten the 'silent majority'. For example, in a recent incident, widely reported in the British press, an Australian comic, Steady Eddy, who has cerebral palsy, was made unwelcome at Tunbridge Wells, the bastion of

Conservative respectability. His performance was cancelled. His manager reflected:

> It's hardly surprising considering the manager was getting calls calling him Satan . . . From my experience in Australia, Steady works anywhere but he tends to draw the working class because they have a more open mind. His humour doesn't work for the upper classes because they can't understand an act with a disability. (Quoted by Ellison, 1994, p. 1)

Having seen Steady Eddy perform at the Edinburgh Festival in August 1994, I would say that he has attracted this level of vitriol because he spits on patronage, is outrageous about disability, celebrates bad-taste humour and delights in discomforting his non-disabled audience. He is also extremely skilful and professional, handling an audience with deft power. None of these features would endear him to a group of listeners who want to hear the voice of pathos, gratitude, subservience and meekness. He is an affront to charity and blatantly bites the hands that feed him.

Hearing New Voices

We can listen but not hear. It is only when these new voices are given *value* within the disability special needs discourses that they will become more widely heard.

In the next chapter I am going to examine the ways in which a vocabulary, use of metaphor and time is being introduced into the language of special needs. In the process, new discourses are emerging, leading the debate into many unexplored areas and opening up exciting opportunities for further discussion. The voices which are now being heard include those of children labelled as having 'special education needs' (Galloway *et al.*, 1994) as well as those of people with profound and multiple disabilities, being expressed through their parents (Fitton, 1994). As consumers of services, they have to be heard far more in the future if we are to pay more than mere lip-service to terms like 'advocacy'.

We also have voices from among the special educators, notably Whittaker (1994), challenging their role in prolonging an out-dated segregated system and promoting change despite opposition. It is important to acknowledge these voices for they are powerful instruments in helping to build and sustain new discourses which re-define special needs.

Listening, in an active way, to the plethora of new voices within the special needs discourses is undeniably taxing. It means there are no more certainties — if we ever assumed that creating terminology was like building a fortress. Special language has always been built on shifting sands. It has never lasted long, as waves move in to wash away one set of words and new shapes are drawn. Let us see it in this way, as a continually changing picture that is re-formed by the elements. There is no value in agonizing over having used redundant terms in the past — they were the only shapes available. We keep learning new words. These new words carry important messages which we need to actively hear if we are to move on productively.

Text 5

What's it got to do with you dear?

Four members of the Integration Alliance (two disabled people, a parent and an ally) staged a small but effective demonstration outside the major national conference on the Draft Code of Practice. We were making the point that Government Officials and non-disabled professionals had yet again organised a 'consultation' on a very important legal document which excluded the voice of consumers.

The conference was held in central London. It cost £65 to attend. It was on a Tuesday day time. No disabled people were invited to speak on the platform, and no national representatives of the Parents Advice Line or Case Work organisations were asked to speak. No free or reduced places were publicly offered to un-sponsored delegates. Over 300 delegates attended, most of whom were funded by their Local Education Authority. This makes a total of £19,500 in ticket money alone. Add to that a day's salary for 300 professionals, the speakers' fees, the hire of halls, the lunch, the advertising, the administration costs, the sum could probably be doubled. £40,000 to put on a show — an illusion of consultation.

Perhaps they were frightened to hear the truth. Unfortunately it is more likely that this is just another example of the Habit of Exclusive Thinking. For decades we disabled people have been seen as perpetual children who don't know what is best for us. Our parents do not fare much better. They are seen as just ordinary people, often guided by emotion not intelligence. It is assumed that they like their children, need to be told what to do, and what to think, by *trained* people. People who know best. So conference after conference is set up to enable the powerful to listen to each other, whilst the disempowered wait outside for instructions.

What to do about this?

In this one case we decided to print a leaflet saying all the uncomfortable things we would have said were we on the platform. We did not ask questions. We gave our best thinking to date, and also made the point about our exclusion. We sat at the doors of the conference and handed out leaflets to as many delegates as we could as they went in. They all seemed to read it. Some chuckled. Some came back to give their approval. Some tried to persuade us to come inside.

When the doors closed we had some coffee together and went home feeling satisfied that we had not agreed to be silenced.

However, national conferences like this will always be 'exclusive' because many disabled people cannot travel long distances and stay in uncomfortable, often inaccessible venues. Likewise, many people with learning difficulties would be excluded by the assumption of reading skills, and the pace of debate. Most parents would be excluded by lack of creche facilities, and all of these people, as well as many more lower paid people, would be excluded by cost. Consultation is part of democracy. We don't know yet how to include everyone's thinking in the forming of policies which affect everybody, but we must keep trying to build new structures, and new methods of communication which bring this goal nearer.

With the television, computer networks, radio, telephone, video, type talk, fax machines all developing new possibilities for connecting person with person across the world, real participation must soon be a possibility.

Grass roots consumer-led organisations should be given

financial support to gather our own opinions and ideas and to represent these views on public platforms.

Summary

The people who use services are often excluded from the design of those services. Professionals are seen as the experts, and they set up ways of asking each other what they think by writing huge, difficult to understand documents, sending them to each other, and inviting and paying for each other to go to conferences to talk about the documents amongst themselves. They call this consultation, but it is not consultation at all. The government will have to find a way to consult with disabled people. (Micheline Mason, *New Learning Together Magazine*, **1**, April 1994)

Questions

1 To what extent does Mason present an example of 'listening' without 'hearing'? Why is it that this well-intentioned audience are unable to hear?
2 What could make this discourse more inclusive?
3 Define the word 'consultation' in its application to this example and in its ideal form.

6 Constructing Different Languages

Introduction

If deconstruction clears the way and disbands the old hierarchies, how can new languages find their form? My approach to this process is to apply a musical analogy for I feel that the creation of language parallels the construction of sounds. I want to ask three questions:

1 Which tunes are now being heard?
2 Is there harmony or discord?
3 Where does this musical style fit?

Unfamiliar sounds take time to hear. They are easy to dismiss. Some perceive the sounds as mere noise. It might even make them feel angry and uncomfortable.

In this chapter, I shall explore the language of 'empowerment'. It is widely employed in relation to special needs. Vulnerable people are said to be empowered through the support of those who service their needs. The disability movement replies that power should be theirs for the taking and that their struggle is with those who ration out portions of the 'empowerment' cake.

My second analogy in this analysis is food related: who decides what we can eat? I use this analogy for two main reasons. Firstly, the apportioning of power is about the one in control of the goodies deciding who is worthy of a second slice and who is too greedy for their own good. Secondly, there has developed a body of literature on 'fat oppression' (e.g., Schoenfielder and Wieser, 1983; Cooper, 1996) which relates to disability politics and introduces new dimensions to the languages of special need.

Finally, in this chapter, I shall speculate on how we might replace that out-dated and, many now feel, offensive term 'special needs' with language which has pride and dignity. Detoxifying the former special language from its traces of paternalism, prejudice and control by establishment values is a daunting challenge. To continue the food metaphor, we are unlikely to rid the substance of all impurities but at least we should be informed of what is potentially risky for us before we decide what to taste.

The Tunes Now Being Heard

There are three dominant tunes being played in the 1990s which will forge the new languages of disability pride in the 21st century. The loudest of these is the social model of disability with its origins in sociological theory. The second tune is played to a civil rights beat, linking disability politics to protest movements for other minority groups and singing for solidarity. The third, more low-key but powerfully melodic, is that which portrays the personal as political in autobiography, art, music, poetry, drama, prose and photography. The three tunes are complimentary yet contrasting. Tune one is theoretical, academic and, to that extent, serves as a 'master narrative'. Tune two is more aggressively staccato but, as in all 'rights-related' discourses, subject to widely differing interpretations. Tune three is emotional, opening up areas of pain, joy, anguish and anger, and, as such, perceived as embarrassingly raw and individualistic by some critics.

Within each of these key discourses are many separate and sometimes conflicting elements. There is no apparent consensus among disabled people as to what music they like to hear played on their behalf. Why should there be? Disabled people vary widely in their level of disability, the extent to which they perceive themselves as disabled and their degree of political consciousness. Many are indifferent to the disability movement whilst some are positively antipathetic towards disability activists. In a society where hierarchies are apparently impregnable, despite public scandals and displays of professional incompetence and establishment corruption there will be those who seek to collude with their oppressors. Why should they bite the hand that feeds them (even if some say they are foolish not to), for powerless people have limited choices.

Where the three tunes join in harmony is their expression of positive images of disability. The social model rejects a 'personal tragedy' image, in which the disabled person is perceived as the problem; the civil rights model promotes collaboration and collective strength as a force for change; the personal as political model illustrates diverse experiences and sharing of feelings which support and validate identity.

Harmony or Discord?

Within these interrelating themes are passages of complexity, contra-diction and challenging enigmas. The special language of the past, with its clear voice from the establishment, was simplistic but relatively unambiguous. It does not do for doctors to express uncertainty. Those who label and categorize are unable to reveal their doubts. The Warnock model operated within an unquestioned class and educational hierar-chy to which we are all expected to aspire and, if sufficiently deserving, to achieve. Within the modernist special language structure, clear and succinct voices could be heard.

These new tunes could produce the most superb harmony, com-bining voices in protest, power, creation and jubilation; they may also produce the most discordant din in conflicting views, in-fighting, strug-gles for dominance and confused messages. The potential for chaos is high. If total discord is the result, then nothing will be heard and no-body is going to listen. The first stage of addressing this dilemma is to explore culture clashes and the fears that have to be faced before cohesion and harmony can be developed.

In an exploration of the relationship between disability politics and gay pride (Corbett, 1994b) I suggested that experiences of dual oppression could lead to the tensions of culture clash. I quoted a poem by Renteria (1993) who expressed her feelings of rejection by different minority communities for belonging to communities they found dis-tasteful. Being rejected by the deaf community for being a lesbian, by the lesbian community for being deaf and by the Hispanic community on both counts adds up to a formidable level of oppression. It is also an illustration of the complexity and contradictions in discourses of marginalized groups. Those who are recipients of prejudice may ex-hibit prejudice against others, as our worldwide conflicts testify.

Torton-Beck expresses her struggles to combat invisibility as both a Jewish woman and a lesbian:

> I would talk to Jewish women about homophobia. I would talk to lesbian groups about anti-semitism, I would talk to both groups about the need to affirm and accept difference. But it has't been that simple, for each group has absorbed some of the myths and distortions about the other without any apparent conscious-ness of irony. (1989, p. xvii)

She speaks of the 'signals of outsiderhood' (*ibid.*) as helping her to be open and affirmative about her identity. One of these 'signals' is that of invisibility, the frightened response to perceived stigma (Goffman, 1968). Where damaging misunderstandings arise is in the absorption of 'myths and distortions' about different stigmatized groups and in the internalizing of guilt and shame. Goffman saw this process as including many diverse groups, among them disabled people and homosexuals.

If harmony and not discord is to prevail, the similarities and not the differences have to be recognized. The greatest obstacle to the establishment of clear, strong voices in the languages that will replace the old, special language is that of fear of exposure, fear of recrimination, fear of being the subject of scorn. This is a fear which fosters mistrust and sets one minority culture against another, creates factions within movements and diminishes power of expression. In exploring the issues of AIDS and cultural politics, for example, Patton says that:

> We are experiencing a dawning recognition that while science constructs our reality, it cannot save us from our human limitations. This is made clear by current cultural and political responses to AIDS, which are at once a throwback to medieval notions of sin and disease, and a confrontation with a cybernetic future of slow viruses and technologised sex. (1989, p. 113)

This deep-seated superstition and fear influences public perceptions of disability and these are magnified in the example of AIDS, where mixed prejudices are fuelled.

For people who have been made invisible, rendered powerless and socially marginalized, there is the damaging paternalism of an establishment which infantalizes them and fails to hear them as adult voices. This is as true for women, black people and the gay community as it is for disabled people. At different stages of recent history, we have all had to claim our adult status from the patriarchal forces which dominate the discourse. Marcus (1992) recalls a magazine essay in the mid-1960s which infantalized gay people as being in a state of arrested development, escaping the responsibilities of life. Such a damaging history of misrepresentation has for so long kept women submissive and child-like and black people prepared to serve in a dependent role. At each historical point of change and revolt, the injured minority group has to reject the dominant interpretation and replace it with their own.

For most people, this finding of an independent voice informed by inner judgment happens in a personal as well as in a collective way. The feminist photographer, Jo Spence said that she would not have been able to offer representations of other people had she not 'first of all begun to explore how I had built a view of myself through other people's representations of me' (1986, p. 83). It is important, in this process of exploration, to recognize from where one is looking. For minority cultures it is from the bottom of the hierarchy: as Dickenson says,

> I have great respect for wisdom, for sight — and these come from being at the bottom. People of colour know whites, women know men, and colonized people know their governors better than those in power know their victims. To oppressors, a victim is only that — not human, not like *us*. (1983, p. 49)

This dismissal of those at the bottom is characteristic of the British establishment, illustrated in Alan Clark's (1994) *Diaries* where his inhumanity towards minority cultures is clearly evident. At the top is the articulate, confident voice of the dominant discourse, whilst at the bottom is the hesitant, frightened confusion of voices unpractised in powerful arenas.

It would be wrong to imply that there are no strong voices emerging in the disability movement beyond those of Oliver and Finkelstein, those of the disabled enlightened modernity. In Morris (1991; 1992) and Shakespeare (1993), there are two powerful and articulate, original voices, creating a more complex and challenging discourse than the three tunes originally played. They can improvise and build patterns of their own volition.

Fitting a Musical Style

Whether it be an unfamiliar prose style, like Kelman's (1994), a discordant sound or a surrealist picture, when new styles of expression emerge they take time to be heard properly. This period of acclimatization might be perceived as a danger zone, during which fragile ideas and images are easily destroyed. In order that a new form of language or languages can replace the old special languages, a climate which accommodates difference needs to be fostered. Just as with new paintings, photography, prose and poetry, any novel means of expression requires new ways of looking, listening and evaluating.

In relation to new special languages, we are moving away from a vocabulary created by professionals, be they medical practitioners, psychologists, therapists or academics, towards one defined and formed by disabled people themselves and supported by allies who seek new means of expression. It seems important to me to recognize that the narratives are going to vary significantly from one cultural group to another, each telling contrasting stories of the same incidents. As Cortazzi says of anthropological models of narrative:

> Social meanings, the social, affective or moral value a narrative may have, is a less obvious aspect of narrative, especially among narrators in a professional group. From this perspective narrative and narrative process will vary enormously in different cultural groups, because people 'talk differently, about different topics, in different ways, to different people, with different consequences' (Barnland, 1975, p. 435). Such differences depend on a group consciousness of norms of speaking and the perception of different abilities, rights, rules, roles and status in communicative situations where narration takes place. Different ways of speaking depend in large part on the social perceptions and interpretations of different cultured groups. (1993, p. 101)

This view of narrative is especially relevant to the widely different language codes used by professional groups — each with their own type of jargon but each able to communicate to the other in a language of privilege — and that used by disabled lay-people and children labelled 'learning difficulty' or 'emotional and behavioral difficulty' and their parents. Where these groups come together in case conferences or in the statementing procedure to determine special educational needs, the divergence in their 'roles and status in communicative situations' (*ibid.*) leads to the dominance of one language over another. Thus the professionals define the terms of reference, set the frame of discourse and disallow discordant language by pushing it out into the margins. Whilst the rhetoric of 'parents as partners' gives their mouthing equal status, the reality of professional dominance sets the vocabulary agenda.

If new special languages are to form their own dominant discourses, representing and reflecting the various elements of disability culture, this will offer a cultural narrative with which the recipients of professional language can identify and use to redefine the terms of reference. This requires that status is given to the language of marginalized groups and that their metaphors are respected. Their ways of seeing will be different from the professionals and it will be easy to dismiss them as inaccurate and unreal. In the struggle with psychiatric diagnosis, this denial of unfamiliar narratives has long been a contentious issue. The fight to have cultural narratives validated is inextricably bound up with the social model of disability, civil rights and the personal as political.

By seeking to analyse special languages through a musical analogy, I have deliberately taken 'special educational needs' out of a narrowly educational context and placed it in a wider arena of those feelings, moods, tones and expectations which pervade every aspect of our daily lives. The 'educational' emphasis, particularly focused since the Warnock Report (1978) and subsequent legislation, has distracted attention from what integration is really about. It is much more than what happens in buildings called schools and colleges; much more than assessment, provision and teaching. It surely concerns the very substance of what constitutes an ethical society which values differences.

One of the key difficulties in the way in which 'integration' has been interpreted, in educational terms, has been that gradations of 'acceptable' disabilities have emerged in the integration hierarchy. Thus, learners with purely physical or sensory disabilities were far more readily integrated than those who presented significant learning or behavioral difficulties. There are 'nice' and 'nasty' special needs: the value judgments being applied have fostered a vocabulary of deviance which keeps certain groups and individuals at the margins. My contention is that unless we face the 'nasty' special needs head on, listen to their cultural narratives and place value on their way of seeing, their residence in the margins will sour and destroy any hope of new languages celebrating difference.

It is valuable to set disability and concepts of 'special needs' in a broad cultural context, in which many marginalized groups have experienced lack of understanding, hostility and patronage from the dominant discourse but have grown to an increased level of power through defining their own terms of reference. In her study of gender and culture at the end of the last century, for example, Showalter (1991) reminds us that women who chose to remain single were labelled 'odd' yet much literature illustrated the power and rhetorical force that their identity gave them. *Anyone* who presents as 'odd' will experience hostility from some quarter. The controversial academic, Camille Paglia (1992), claims that she was regarded as 'odd' among her own academic community for being too loud and outrageous — as if she is in show business rather than academia. This is about taste as well: do we only want our social oddities in good taste? Does 'proud to be odd' cause offence?

Indeed, it is only relatively recently that we, as a society, have perceived disabled people and especially those with learning disabilities, as sexual beings — in other words, as real adults with adult needs. This is important to recognize if we are to hear their voices and respect them. The pattern of paternalistic discourses speaking for them will only be truly challenged when we see them as whole beings, not as vulnerable innocents who need care. The establishment attitude to disability has been informed by an image of the 'deserving poor', begging for charity and grateful for whatever hand-outs they receive. It is the 'niceness' that, is being rewarded. I would want us to ask, 'How different is "difference"?' To what extent can we expose the real humanity and still retain acceptance of difference? Is it acceptable for some disabled people, as Taylor (1991) describes, to enjoy the benefits that prostitutes can offer them? Do we extend the concepts of 'special needs' to include people, like those in the notorious 'spanner' case, who enjoy sado-masochism as a form of pleasurable play yet are prosecuted for their break of public acceptance of difference (Thompson, 1994)? If we move away from just tolerating the 'nice' part of 'special needs', then we are really listening to different tunes rather than hearing what we want to hear.

Empowerment or Destruction?

Empowerment seems to me to be redolent of the slave trade — in relating to clear hierarchies of power — and this makes a direct impact on language use. The language that those being 'empowered' are used to using is deferential. Gordon (1902) gives an example from the language used in 'the old quarter' of the deep south of America at the end of the last century when assessing 'negro dialect' where the use of 'Ol' Master' and 'Ol' Miss' was commonplace. For disabled people and those categorized as having special needs there is a similar inbuilt language of deference towards professionals, especially the medical profession. They have been conditioned to listen to the voice of authority, to respect the language which defines their role and status, their limitations and potential, to observe the time limits for questioning very important people.

Becoming Visible

Engelberg refers to those whose feelings of disconnectedness make them believe they are 'orphaned by history' (1989, p. 19) and suffer anxieties of lack of influence: making no mark on what is recorded as human achievement and expression. This sense of loss and isolation is a key feature of the state of disempowerment and is particularly pronounced where fear of appearing 'odd' makes individuals seek invisibility. When the language of empowerment is used in relation to people with 'special educational needs', it is about helping them to increase their visibility. Yet the process of 'coming out' into a vocal and assertive identity can be extremely threatening and stressful. This is where empowerment is about grossly unequal demands. The powerful, with the confidence of authority, are in a position to proffer power of expression; the powerless have their faltering attempts at speaking new languages (i.e., the language of those in power) exposed as inept and confused. It can result in a destruction of confidence and a longing for the old invisibility.

Too Much is Bad for You

How much power should be given to the powerless? This perennial dilemma in educational ethics has long been applied to class, gender and race. There have always been certain sections of society that have been allowed just so much learning and only a restricted entry into the dominant discourses by a fearful and wary establishment.

The notion of 'self-advocacy' for disabled people, and particularly for those with learning disabilities, is a central element of their empowerment. It is about giving them the space to speak and to contribute to the dominant discourses on disability. Their powerlessness has been compounded by long-established attitudes towards 'mental deficiency' which saw them as sub-human. They are not used to being listened to or having their perceptions valued. Often they have considerable difficulties in expressing ideas and feelings, being accustomed to others speaking on their behalf.

There is now an increased recognition that people with learning disabilities are a very vulnerable group, open to exploitation and abuse. Their language is one which is devalued; the words they use are not given equal weight to those in the dominant discourse. In current research in Britain, the cases of physical and sexual abuse among this group are discovered to be higher than anticipated (Craft, 1994). The realization is that, until these voices were acknowledged and their mouthing actually believed, what happened to them went unnoticed.

Advocacy support groups, given names like 'Voice' help people with learning disabilities to express their feelings and wishes. In a recent radio programme (Radio 4, 3rd November 1994) different voices were heard talking about the physical and sexual abuse of a particular man with learning disabilities. The listeners heard a sympathetic male nurse, a distressed mother and a defensive hospital manager. Each reflected their own language cultures using words and images which presented their individual interpretations of events. What is clearly evident is that those who have been silent and silenced for so long are creating extreme discomfort within the establishment. Dominant medical discourses are being challenged, by the voices of those with learning disabilities and their advocates. Their perceptions are being heard and no longer dismissed as fantasy or the ramblings of confused minds.

Even people who are unable to speak and who experience multiple disabilities are expressing their needs through their advocates and carers (Fitton, 1994). There is no longer any excuse for those in the dominant disability discourses to dismiss the recipients of services as invisible, mute and passive. Yet there is still a compulsion among those used to their language being the most highly valued to 'teach the dumb to speak': to place their interpretation on new languages because they are unfamiliar, strange and often threatening.

As the disability movement has gained strength in the discourses, it has become abrasive in attacking the dominant language of professional power and categorization. The language 'for' disabled people is rejected. It has to be as much 'of' disabled people as possible — even if this involves changing the membership of discourse arenas — pushing the old voices into the margins, forcing a new, angry presence.

Inevitably, this struggle for the disability discourse is stressful and creates tensions and pain. For those who felt they had been devotedly speaking up for disabled people, there is the pain of feeling displaced and misunderstood. This can create an angry backlash. Some of those who were used to having their words respected and unchallenged display scepticism and hostility to what they perceive as 'too much' empowerment. It is alright to let people develop space in the discourse if they are then to make constructive comments. When they use this space to begin the process of deconstruction, dislodging the old certainties, reinterpreting the established metaphors and building entirely novel patterns of language hierarchies, this is potentially a source of all-out warfare.

What an adherence to 'empowerment' has unleashed is a source of conflicts and the settling of old scores. Where people have felt oppressed for years by a weight of professional tyranny in deciding what they are, where they should go, and which category they can be placed into, the accumulated anger is considerable. The old power relations are still firmly in situ, however. The powerless are speaking but in a language which is still spoken and understood by few in authority.

De-toxifying Special Language

If we acknowledge that the dominant disability discourses are not going to be destroyed entirely by the inclusion of new languages, how can they be gradually rid of their most damaging aspects? The most valuable approach might be to filter in new words and concepts which subtly and significantly change the old discourses. An all-out takeover is unlikely. The unequal starting points would mean that the new languages will always be kept at the edge, allowed so much expression but no more. But if words like 'special' are to be made redundant, this has to involve a major reconceptualization of what constitutes humanity. Diversity and difference need to be valued and celebrated. Then we all become special; yet none of us is so special that we are more or less than human.

The old discourses need to de-toxify themselves. They can only do this through a process of intensive and receptive *listening*. As there will be sounds which are so unfamiliar as to appear little more than silences, this listening is extremely difficult. In order that words and images free themselves for reinterpretation, the mood needs to be one of improvised risk-taking; letting language work loose, float and reform in unconscious patterns. It requires courage and humility: courage, to recognize that old ways of speaking and conceptualizing may have to go for ever; and humility, to stand down from the old hierarchies and relinquish language power.

The analogy for this receptivity to de-toxification is that of jazz improvisation. In a session of musical creativity and expression, each sound is distinctive, of equal value and contributes to the whole. The fusion of sound produces a joint harmony. Above all, there is a concentration on *active listening* in order that each can respond to the other, picking up each sound and building upon what is heard. The process of de-toxifying special languages as it currently exists calls for new ways of listening to the many voices now speaking in many tongues.

Back to Bad-mouthing

I want to return to the image with which I began, in order to reflect on continuity and change. In 'Teaching the Dumb to Speak', my 1871 choice of frontispiece, we see the formally dressed male instructor placing his hands on the young deaf girl's hand and wrist to ensure that she conforms to what is expected of her in the drive for oralism. This is a poignant image for us to consider, for it embodies the concept of dominant discourses overwhelming all other forms of expression. It says to us, 'speak our language and we will listen; speak your own and we are not going to make the effort to hear you'.

In the analogy that I have applied to constructing new languages, it is in the silent spaces in improvised jazz where deaf people now speak. In those silent spaces, we must concentrate to listen. Sign language contains a vocabulary rich in dynamic expression. Through it, deaf people can usually say things that they would find very difficult to express orally. Yet, most of us are unable to 'speak' this language and remain reluctant to learn it. It is not the dominant discourse and requires too much effort from us.

What we need to learn more than anything else, if we are to construct and sustain a rich diversity of languages, is to break away from narrow conceptions of what constitutes 'language'. There are many different forms of expressing ideas, feelings and preferences. One of the forms is in sign language, including Makaton signing which is used by some people with learning disabilities. However, there are other people with learning disabilities who communicate through facial expression, eye contact and body language. They may have no verbal sounds and no signing. How do we listen to their languages? Are they trying to say anything to us or should we simply speak for them?

When I worked with children who spoke through facial expression, eye contact and body language, they gradually taught me how to interpret their languages. I learnt to 'hear' their discomfort, anger, distress, excitement or delight. Their individual preferences were expressed by them, if I was prepared to 'listen' carefully and not to impose my values on their experiences. It is about listening to silent spaces. The effort required is considerable, yet I cannot see what 'empowerment' means unless we are prepared to concentrate on *really* hearing one another. What is often referred to as empowering, I fear, is nothing more than an introduction to the dominant discourse and an invitation to join in. This can only lead to a subtle form of language colonization, whereby those able to assimilate language codes are included and those who resist or find the process unmanageable are regarded as 'other'.

Whatever form our language takes, the importance of self-expression is overwhelming. It is what makes us human. Rodenburg, in discussing our need for a form of words, speaks of expression 'becoming part of our circulatory system, touching every part of us. It articulates our most vital needs as a human being' (1993, p. 3). What she refers to as 'words' can be more broadly applied to the range of languages which include both signing and body language.

The tyranny for most disabled people in recent years has been in their exclusion from dominant discourses. In the medical and psychological discourses of diagnosis and assessment, their voices used to be silent. They were not heard and, therefore, misunderstood and misrepresented, as Rodenburg says:

> We can get lost when we roam too long within the folds of silence. Our feelings have no means of being charted, our ideas stay stunted and unclear, our personalities remain confused and inexplicit. Words make the world coherent. (1993, p. 12)

The power of language is such that disability politics will only compliment and challenge dominant disability discourses as its speakers become more practised and confident, creating their own metaphors and extending the vocabulary for other discourses to adopt.

Conclusion

In this chapter I have reflected on the ways in which new languages are emerging, marginalized discourses are moving towards the centre, and new ways of listening give space for construction. I concluded with a return to the concept of 'Bad-mouthing' — the imposition which the dominant discourse makes on the marginalized.

As I move to the next, and concluding, chapter of this book I want to consider the ways in which we read and hear texts. Our discourses are founded on texts and sustained by them. The relationship between the written and spoken word is one of interdependency and responsiveness. Within this process there are key texts which emerge and influence the discourses over a considerable period. Goffman is a good example of a writer whose texts relating to the disability culture have continued to be debated, revised, rejected, reshaped but not ignored. In *Asylums* (Goffman, 1961) he produced a text which the psychiatric profession continues to use to evaluate the unintended consequences of the processes of which they are a central part (Manning, 1992). His analysis has been used to serve as a platform for subsequent research initiatives on institutionalization and its effects (e.g., Baron, 1987), creating an ongoing dialogue on the issues he raised.

The power discourse has its roots in the class structure where elites rule through a confident and calculated manipulation of imagery. If new languages are to be accorded status and, thereby, listened to with respect, they need to manipulate the imagery of the dominant discourse and replace out-moded metaphors. One of the most effective ways in which this can occur is in literary forms, where artistic expressions or witty anecdotes create new and memorable images. The radical psychiatrist, Szasz, offers particularly powerful examples of this:

> In hospital psychiatry, the best way to tell the patient from the psychiatrist is by who has the keys; in nonhospital psychiatry, by who has the *key words*. (1991, p. 55, my emphasis)

> Religion and the jargon of the helping/hindering professions are comprised largely of *literalized metaphors*. That is why they are the perfect tools for legitimizing and illegitimizing ideas, behaviours and persons. (1991, p. 57, my emphasis)

There is a struggle for key words. Through them ideas and behaviours are indeed legitimized to become part of an established creed. The language of special needs, if radically deconstructed, can become the languages of many sources of expression, sharing a space and listening, arguing and forming metaphors which provide new tools for ideas. A diffusion of the old power structures is a step towards dignity for those whose perceptions have long been devalued.

Text 6

You Have to be Deaf to Understand

What is it like to 'hear' a hand?
You have to be deaf to understand!

What is it like to be a small child
In a school, in a room void of sound —
With a teacher who talks and talks and talks;
And then when she does come around to you,
She expects you to know what she's said?
You have to be deaf to understand.

Or the teacher who thinks that to make you smart,
You must first learn how to talk with your voice:
So mumbo-jumbo with hands on your face
For hours and hours without patience or end,
Until out comes a faint resembling sound?
You have to be deaf to understand.

What is it like to be curious,
To thirst for knowledge you can call your own,
With an inner desire that's set on fire . . . ,
And you ask a brother, sister, or friend
Who looks in answer and says, 'Never mind!'?
You have to be deaf to understand.

What is it like in a corner to stand,
Though there's nothing you've done really wrong,
Other than try to make use of your hands
To a silent peer to communicate
A thought that comes to your mind all at once?
You have to be deaf to understand.

What is it like to be shouted at
When one thinks that will help you to hear;
Or misunderstand the words of a friend
Who is trying to make a joke clear,
And you don't get the point because he's failed?
You have to be deaf to understand.

What is it like to be laughed in the face
When you try to repeat what is said;
Just to make sure that you've understood,
And you find that the words were misread . . .
And what you want to cry out 'Please help me, friend!'?
You have to be deaf to understand.

What is it like to have to depend
Upon one who can hear to phone a friend;
Or place a call to a business firm
And be forced to share what's personal, and
Then find that your message wasn't made clear?
You have to be deaf to understand.

What is it like to be deaf and alone
in the company of those who can hear —
And you only guess as you go along.
For no-one's there with a helping hand,
as you try to keep up with words and song?
You have to be deaf to understand.

What is it like on the road of life
To meet with a stranger who opens his mouth . . .
And speaks out a line at a rapid pace;
And you can't understand the look in his face
Because it is new and you're lost in the race?
You have to be deaf to understand.

What is it like to comprehend
Some nimble fingers that paint the scene,
And make you smile and feel serene
With the 'spoken word' of the moving hand
That makes you part of the world at large?
You have to be deaf to understand.

What is it like to 'hear' a hand?

Yes, you have to be deaf to understand!
(*William J. Madsen*)

Questions

1 If you look at the frontspiece, 'Teaching the Dumb to Speak', and then read this poem, what do you feel is being expressed by the question, 'What is it like to "hear" a hand?'

2 If it is true that 'you have to be deaf to understand', what do you think this is telling us about the limits of empathy? What is it saying about disability discourses and their level of significance?

3 Have people in marginalized discourses been 'shouted at'? In what respects do you think that 'shouted at' could be a metaphor for professional arrogance?

Conclusion

In my introductory chapter I stated that my intention in this book was to focus upon the influence of new discourses, personal narratives and the use of metaphor. To conclude, I shall reflect upon these elements in relation to textual analysis, the characteristic features of the language of special needs and the personal as political. The tone of this book is one which deliberately seeks to combine the disparate aims of encouraging a critical evaluation of existing, published texts with a fostering of introspection and personal reflection. It is important to me that we both explore what is defined as being 'real' in terms of special needs or disability culture and, alongside this, we look to our own cultural status and perceptions of self needs. The examination of one without the other serves to perpetuate the distancing of 'otherness'.

Reviewing the Texts

In reviewing the six texts that have been presented through the preceding chapters, I shall explore the extent to which the linking of legacies is evident or, alternatively, the breaking of bonds is illustrated. The 'educational' emphasis is only obliquely referred to within all but the first text from Warnock. This is an attempt, on my part, to remove 'special needs' from a narrowly focused arena into a much wider cultural context. Among the six texts, there are none which are characteristically 'academic' in style. Even the Warnock extract is simple and direct in its use of language and includes none of the familiar references and use of academic jargon that can alienate the lay reader. In several of the texts, there is a direct, forceful and personal style, more redolent of journalism than academia. I have deliberately not selected either specifically educational texts, which relate to details of practice, or theoretical texts which present special education debates. This is a book about the relationship between the language of special education and the language of disability culture, the discourses which have emerged, and their key features. These texts are, therefore, reflecting the diversity of language which is found within the complexity of disability culture.

Text 1 is written in a clear and confident style. It is the reflection of Mary Warnock, who chaired the committee of enquiry into the education of *Handicapped Children and Young People* (DES, 1978) in Britain. On the face of it, this appears to be a morally ethical stance which is being taken, to develop a concept of educational needs to counteract the effects of inequalities and disadvantage. As such, it cannot be seen as retrograde or damaging. It is a move forward from past legislation. The style and form demonstrate the calm, cool confidence of enlightened modernity. There is an air of authority and measured strength in the tone of this piece. It is impersonal, yet the 'we' implies a secure consensus.

Text 2 is intensely personal and, in contrast to the tone of calm security in text 1, it reflects uncertainty and an eager, excited quest for confirmation of positive identity. This text offers an illustration of the rich diversity offered by disability arts — the imagery and political expression. Alison Silverwood has selected a range of performers and artists on the disability arts scene in Britain whose work demonstrates the two major strands of disability culture; the impact of creative expression to show ways of being and the reality of a disabled identity. In her presentation of one particular performer, Char March, the tensions of dual oppression are explored. She quotes Char as saying, 'I want to be an iceberg / to gash / an unstoppable hole / in their complacency' (1994, p. 4). This is a powerful metaphor for much of what is reflected on the disability arts circuit. Within the language of the disabled performers can be found a high level of aggression, sarcasm, bitterness and cynicism. Silverwood refers to this reflectively:

> Making people feel uncomfortable is a dangerous way to get across political ideas — the defensiveness can be boring — but amongst the shuffling and squirming I'm sure intellectual light bulbs pop on. (*ibid.*)

Her observation raises interesting issues about disability culture, including: How far can provocation be pushed before it becomes tedious?

The language of disability arts mirrors the conflicting discourses debated in the earlier chapters. Whilst the enlightened modernity of text 1 is courteous and presents the voice of reason, the voices heard in text 2 are often unreasonable and belligerent. It is about rationality being confronted with anarchy. In the example of Char, she is challenging the cosy image of special need, the acceptable face of passivity, gratitude and stereotypical physical dependency. Mental illness is an uncomfortable disability, definitely not 'cosy' and, when coupled within sexual deviance, it is a challenge to the 'niceness' which I discussed in relation to concepts of 'special'. One of the great strengths of disability arts, as I see it, is that it confronts 'niceness' and relishes the 'nasty' bits, forcing the audience to see disabled people as fully developed human beings and not one dimensional, charity, cut-out figures, ever smiling with arms out-stretched. One of the dangers, though, is that this political approach to artistic expression risks a backlash of rejection and impatience from an audience who seek entertainment first and doctrine second. The balance, therefore, has to be delicate and carefully tuned. To return to the musical analogy, discordant sounds are stimulating and challenging but need to be tempered with some gentle and melodic interludes.

Text 3 offers an interesting example of 'empowerment', in which deaf, gay people take ownership of the language. The tone and style of Raymond Luczak's prose reflects the more assertive and confident voices of disability activists in America. Whereas there is an evident aggression in much of the British disability rights polemic, the American movement appears to have moved on from aggression to confident assertion. The selection of the three key words — 'paternalism', 'homophobia' and 'audism' — as concepts to be aware of in a move to increased self-empowerment, links broader cultural differences with the legacy of the medical model. The tyranny of 'paternalism' and 'audism' is illustrated in the picture that opens this book. There is a clear image of fostering speech to alleviate 'dumbness'. Luczak offers both a challenge to the medical model of disability and to the voice of enlightened modernity. Linking the prejudices towards deafness to those towards gay people is a powerful indicator of the thinly concealed undercurrent of hatred which relates to 'special needs'. The example of a 'cochlea implant operation' presents the reader with a challenge to the medical model of disability. This kind of intervention and 'cure' is seen by the general public as beneficial. Luczak seems to be suggesting that it should be recognized as a rejection of differences, and that it is as potentially damaging to self-esteem as the efforts in the recent past to 'cure' the disease of homosexuality.

Shapiro's text, text 4, is perhaps the most academic of those presented for analysis, as it seeks to evaluate the growth and development of the disability movement in America. He is offering a non-disabled author's reflections and, as can be seen in the extract, he goes to considerable efforts to ensure that his text includes a rich diversity of voices which reflect disability culture. It is interesting that, whilst he quotes the editor of a well-known American journal, *The Disability Rag*, there has been criticism of his book from that same source. In the March/April 1995 edition, Xenia Williams complains that, although *No Pity* presents positive images of most disabilities, 'it trashes the crazies' (p. 8). Her challenge reflects the very real difficulties inherent in multiple discourses. It is a feature of what I explored earlier in divergent voices presenting the risk of chaos, confusion and a struggle for dominance. 'Mental illness' alongside 'learning disabilities' remains a poor relation of other disabilities whose voices are more clearly recognized to represent disability culture generally. The deliberate embracing of 'bad taste' language, like 'cripple' or 'crazies', is a way in which disabled people have taken ownership of the language that describes them. It reflects humour and proud assertion, the fostering of a raw and naked discourse to challenge and affront the dominant discourses of medicine, psychology and education. It offers a personal and honest interpretation of reality, taking words that could be offensive if used by those outside the discourse and making them symbols of a cohesive identity.

Text 5, by Micheline Mason, is from a radical educational journal recently published in Britain, which advocates an inclusive approach to education and community living. It neatly encapsulates the tensions between the old discourses and the new. There are the professionals, speaking 'for' disabled people, dominating the public space as well as the discourse arena, while Mason and her small group, marginalized and apparently forgotten, are unable to participate in a 'real' consultation. It is the old rhetoric of 'empowerment' at work again. The enormous advantages of networking, common language codes and financial power, as personified in the professional discourse, are demonstrably unequal to the marginalized, dependent status of the consumers of services. The drawing offers a powerful image of this imbalance of power. Like the 'Teaching the Dumb to Speak' drawing, it provides a vivid illustration of the fragility and fraudulence of much which goes by the name of 'empowerment'. Both pictorial images are saying, 'You can enter our discourse arena on our terms, if you wish. We give you the freedom to do so.' This is a painfully restricted version of empowerment, as Mason indicates. It mocks democracy. As a means of consultation, it cannot be said to encourage critical reflection.

Text 6, the final text in this book, is a poem about the experience of deafness which takes us back to where we began with 'Teaching the Dumb to Speak'. The poem, written by a Professor of English at the famous American University for deaf students, Gallaudet, is now over 20 years old. Yet it contains language and metaphors which offer distinctive features of disability discourses. 'What is it like to "hear" a hand?' he asks us. 'You have to be deaf to understand.' What this poem portrays most effectively is the frustration and pain of feeling locked into a language code which isolates you from the dominant discourses and which is undervalued or held in contempt. The importance of being able to communicate is overwhelming, forging identity, self-esteem and collective strength. So many strands of the disability discourses remain muted because the dominant discourse of diagnosis, assessment and categorization cannot hear. The 'faint, resembling sound' of deaf people being forced to vocalize can be seen to serve as a metaphor for the degree of impact which disability culture can make on the dominant discourses when driven to speak their jargon. It is a poem which reflects the real differences between 'special needs' languages and the hierarchy of privileged discourse which is perpetuated by professional interest and an incapacity to listen with sufficient intensity and humility.

To summarize, the key issues to emerge from a review of the texts included in this book.

1   There is a linking legacy of struggle against the dominant discourse of enlightened modernity and professional patronage.
2   The diverse strands of disability culture lead to divergent and sometimes conflicting discourses.
3   Aggression is moving towards assertion, led by the American Disability Rights Movement, making the language proud and confident.
4   The variety and scope of these new discourses requires a new kind of listening, prepared to value the meanings of unfamiliar sounds.
5   It is not necessarily in educational or theoretical texts where the disability discourses will be found, but in poetry, drama and personal narrative.

After Postmodernism, Then ... ?

By presenting Warnock and similar 'sacred' texts as the voices of enlightened modernity, in contrast to the plurality of disability discourses, I have explored the ways in which a postmodernist analysis might be applied to the language of special needs. Adair refers to two of the more high-minded faces of postmodernism as being 'the innovatory and the archival' (1992, p. 17). This interpretation seems apt in relation to special language, where we have the historical development of a word bank of diagnosis, definition and application of treatment, informing us of the cultural context from which this vocabulary emerged. To challenge this privileged archive, the plethora of disability discourses, often in the form of poems, paintings, photographs and songs, presents innovative signs and symbols. In text 5, we see the disabled participant being alienated from the professional forum with 'What's it got to do with you dear?' Adair suggests that the traditional congregational forms, from theatre or opera-houses to meeting places and conferences, will be changed in the postmodern world, where it will 'no longer be a question of congregation but of circulation, no longer of venues but of avenues' (1992, p. 20). I find this an attractive and exciting concept, offering, as it does, a potential for cultural fluidity and cross-fertilization of new ways of seeing, located in diverse arenas.

Rubin Suleiman reminds us of the critical appraisal of postmodernist approaches, which equate this movement with 'the cultural exhaustion of late capitalism, or of the decay produced by the proliferation of mass culture' (1994, p. 227). This implies a negative view of the confusion and uncertainty created by changes in the central arena. She summarizes the tensions within this debate by suggesting that,

> The universalist (or, if you will, modernist) claim is that only by ascribing universal validity to one's ethical beliefs is one able to act ethically. A postmodernist ethics refuses to take that step, arguing that such ascriptions merely elevate one set of contingent beliefs to 'universal' status and that too many horrors have been inflicted by some human beings on others in the name of *their* universal values. (pp. 231–2)

Taking her definition of postmodernist ethics, I shall apply it to two examples from the archives of special language, in order to conclude this exploration with a critical re-appraisal of the impact of universal values.

Teaching the Dumb to Speak: Defining Power, Defining Weakness

In the history of deaf education we have perhaps the most dramatic example of the application of universal values upon a cultural minority. There was no doubt among those early educators in the nineteenth century that they thought that they knew what was best. As this American expert stated,

I have seen within the last year, impromptu conversational English used by deaf-born pupils of the Northampton, Rochester and Philadelphia schools, in a manner to lead me to hope that the day is near at hand when the deaf-born, in general, will go forth from these schools, and from many others, able to comprehend *the full force of our language*, prepared to use it in the intercourse of life, and fitted to go forward in the independent acquisition of knowledge. Indeed, rare minds among them may carry *the golden key to the paradise of literature*. (Gordon, 1892, p. xv, my emphasis)

This universal discourse, like that of Warnock, implies that there is a single track to educational fulfilment, whereby *they* can join *our* language and *our* literature. In a later re-appraisal of such an emphasis, Lane embraces the richness of difference when he says that,

The renewed appreciation of cultural pluralism in our society today invites us to re-examine the conviction that others should speak as we do. Many Americans can recall their initial shock when they realized fully for the first time that other people were conducting their lives in an entirely different language. Perhaps that shock reflects a kind of egocentrism that it is in our common interest to overcome, for the growth of social consciousness, like that of the child, is largely a series of triumphs over egocentrism. (1984, p. 12)

I like this analogy, for it reflects the fear and hatred of difference which permeates special language and it accentuates the need to move beyond assimilation. Teaching approaches in relation to deaf learners were, historically, dependent upon images of otherness as Fay indicates when he refers to a process of language acquisition as helping 'to transfer the deaf-mute from his condition as a foreigner, to that of one *to the manner born* (1893, p. 35, my emphasis). The use of such language suggests a class hierarchy of cultural dominance, whereby the use of anything other than the privileged discourse renders the user as outside the boundaries, beyond the limits of power and therefore in a silent space.

Within the archives of language relating to learning disability, we can find many instances of universal values which inflict horrors on others. In a medical text of the 1960s, only a few years outside our cultural history, we can see 'weakness' described as being the most negative characteristic of 'subnormal personalities' (Earl, 1961). The 'weak' individuals used as case-study examples in this text are generally of a fairly high level of capability, as measured by the psychological tests then in use, but are mostly described as demonstrating a degree of apathy, inertia and lack of persistence. Many of them are also defined in the text as being 'over-institutionalised'. The moral stance taken against their inherent deficiencies is patently an imposition of universal ethical values upon pluralism. Earl concludes his discussion on 'weakness' with this reflection:

> In conclusion it must be insisted that weakness is the gravest single defect in any inadequate personality. The immature may become mature, the unstable may stabilise, the unintelligent be slowly trained, the schizoid, athetoid, neurotic, may adjust; but the really weak are doomed. (1961, p. 85)

The fundamentalist fervour of such a moral judgment puts into perspective the equally fanatical use of language in some examples from the various disability discourses of the 1990s. As Walter (1994) says of fundamentalism in any form, it offers us something to stand on, beliefs and confirmation of the validity of our reasoning and, therefore, it reflects diverse ideological factions. When re-evaluating the special language of the past, we need to try and understand the context it came from and to confront the concepts and metaphors both in the language of others and in our own mouthings.

From Invisibility to Pride: The Power of Bad-mouthing

As a key element of this book, I have chosen to incorporate personal narrative into my analysis. Perhaps one of the major deficiencies of the language is that of naming the recipients of services, those with 'needs', as 'other'. What I have learned, in my own reflections of personal growth, is to recognize the 'other' inside myself and to relish this sense of acceptance.

Hevey (1992), in his vivid account of the richness that 'coming out' from invisibility to a proud disabled identity gave to him, demonstrates the strength which such a process provides. My own experience was that of submerging and, thus, making invisible my sexual identity as a lesbian. Such a destructive act led to a nervous breakdown at the age of twenty-one, where my internal distress expressed itself in outbursts of panic and extreme anxiety. It interests me now, with the healing benefit of hindsight, that this coincided with my first year of teaching, where I was to progress to a career in special education. In a recent paper (Corbett, 1996), I re-evaluated my teaching experiences and asked myself if I needed the special education system as much, if not more, than it needed me. For me, it offered a chance to help other vulnerable people and, in so doing, gave comfort and stability to myself. I have found this return to my early career choices a valuable experience, for it has helped me, as a theorist now as well as a past practitioner, to question the concept of 'need' and to challenge notions of what constitutes 'special'. Perhaps there were other frightened practitioners, like myself, who gained assurance from their daily contact with a 'safe' form of specialness.

When I came out as a lesbian, five years ago, it was because of an unbearable tension of falsehood, a defeatism and despair, a desperate depression. At that stage, I could not have called it pride. That has only come with the strength that an open and receptive approach to life can bring. One of the most valuable developments for my personal growth has been in being able to acknowledge that I have survived mental ill-health and that I can now celebrate my feelings of well-being. As an active member of Survivors' Poetry, a group which was founded in 1991 to provide poetry workshops and performances by and for survivors of the mental health system, I have been able to use the power of language to express my pride in confronting life's challenges. Recently, I performed two of my poems at a Survivors' Poetry Presentation. One was from that bleak period in 1969 when I was a distressed twenty-one year old. It is about invisibility, and says,

> Ceasing as a whole
> I rupture into tiny twigs.
> I fear these twigs might splinter —
> Such fragile limbs.
> Twine-twisted, I sneeze
> With every wisp of breeze.
> If I stand very still
> Maybe nobody will see. (9 March 69)

My urge to become inanimate was very strong at that time and I can remember the feeling of being inside a perpetual play where I was continually speaking other people's lines. The recent poem I read, by contrast, was confident and calm. It suggested that, in times of stress, we can,

> Just rise above it
> Lift your mind out

Let it float away
From all this crap
Leave go and skim
High on another plane.
Sometimes believe me,

I rise so far
Touch soaring birds
Roll giddy into clouds.
Then nothing touches you
You breathe slow and deep
and only sink when ready.
Rising above is good for the soul
I recommend it.

(from 'Rising Above it' in *Under the
Asylum Tree*, 1995, p. 37)

If I try to view this poem dispassionately, as an example of the language of disability culture, then I might suggest that it demonstrates both the power of creativity to transcend negative experiences and the value of confronting everyday lived realities. We can all too easily 'bad-mouth' ourselves, when we are faced with set-backs. If we learn to 'rise above', we can use this as a coping strategy to detach from negativity. I hasten to add that, whilst I see the value of this in theory, I often fail to apply it effectively in practice!

Ways Forward: Opening the Language Debate

One of the difficulties for those of us who, for whatever reason, feel outside the central discourses is that we remain ill-identified when we defy definition by the modernist doctrine. Bauman (1992) describes this interestingly as the 'pilgrims' of modernism, with their life-plan journey, as opposed to the 'nomads' of postmodernism/deconstruction who remain nebulous in identity. He suggests that,

> The nomads, like the pilgrims, were all along busy constructing their identities; but theirs were 'momentary' identities, identities 'for today' until-further notice identities. Nomads do not bind the time/space, they move through it; and so they move through identities. (1992, p. 167)

This notion of moving through identities challenges inflexible definitions of normality. The disability rights lobby (e.g., *London Disability News*, GLAD, March 1995) rejects the universal values of 'normal life' imposed on them by government. If we avoid defining what constitutes 'normal', we risk annoying those who feel the anxiety of critical scrutiny challenging the old familiar language codes. Mark Lawson writing in the *Independent* newspaper in January 1995, expresses discomfort at the level of 'edgy self scrutiny' experienced by white, male writers when faced with the 'spraying of fashionable air-fresheners in the cultural atmosphere' (p. 15). It is all too easy to retreat into a crude attack on the barbarism of political correctness when confronted with other ways of seeing: such a process requires a level of humility which has to shrink the egocentric approach.

One of the characteristic features of postmodernist thinking is its playfulness. As one who has come late to valuing play, I see its strength in helping us to refresh our senses, explore and take risks. Perhaps the ways forward, for special educators, lie in practices which include elements of the following:

1 Probing the depths of texts to tease out surprising aspects (e.g., Sanger, 1995).
2 Recognizing the personal value judgments which define the language of individual need (e.g., Silin, 1993).
3 Acknowledging the human in all beings, with its potential for good and ill, without isolating 'special' as 'nice' (e.g., Waite, 1995).
4 Addressing the dilemma of professional knowledge as an intractable struggle of progression and re-evaluation (e.g., Hoyle and John, 1995).

One thing of which we can be certain is that the 'politically correct' language we now feel comfortable with in 1996 will appear crudely insensitive and inappropriate by the year 2010. Perhaps we can comfort ourselves with the thought that, if we are able to 'move through' identities, we can also adopt a similar approach to the use of special language. Maybe if there are more 'nomads' filling the central arena the plurality of discourses will make all language special. Thus 'special' becomes normality.

Bibliography

ABBERLEY, P. (1987) 'The concept of oppression & the development of a social theory of disability', *Disability, Handicap & Society*, **2**, 1, pp. 5–20.

ACKER, S. (1994) *Gendered Education*, Milton Keynes, Open University Press.

ADAIR, G. (1992) *The Post-Modernist Always Rings Twice; Reflections on Culture in the 90s*, London, Fourth Estate Limited.

AINSCOW, M. and TWEDDLE, D. (1979) *Preventing Classroom Failure: An Objective Approach*, Chichester, John Wiley & Sons.

AINSCOW, M. (1989) 'How should we respond to individual needs?', in AINSCOW, M. and FLOREK, A. (eds) *Special Educational Needs: Towards a Whole School Approach*, London, David Fulton.

BAILEY, R. (1994) 'A tale of a bubble', in KEITH, L. (ed.) *Mustn't Grumble*, London, The Women's Press.

BALL, S. (1994) *Education Reform*, Milton Keynes, Open University Press.

BAMLUND, D.C. (1975) *Private and Public Self in Japan and the United States*, Tokyo, Simul Press.

BARON, C. (1987) *Asylum to Anarchy*, London, Free Association Books.

BARTLEY, G. (1871) *The Schools for the People*, London, Bell & Daldy.

BARTON, L. (ed.) (1988) *The Politics of Special Educational Needs*, London, Falmer Press.

BAUMAN, Z. (1992) *Mortality, Immortality and Other Life Strategies*, Cambridge, Polity Press.

BEGUM, N. (1994) 'Mirror, mirror on the wall', in BEGUM, N., HILL, M. and STEVENS, A. (eds) *Reflections: The Views of Black Disabled People on Their Lives & Community Care*, London, Central Council for Education and Training in Social Work.

BENDER, M. (1976) 'Special education', in JOHNSTON, R. and MAGRALS, P. (eds) *Developmental Disorders: Assessment, Treatment, Education*, Baltimore, University Press.

BILLEN, A. (1994) 'The life interview', *Observer*, July 24, p. 10.

BOOTH, T. (1981) 'Demystifying integration', in SWANN, W. (ed.) *The*

Practice of Special Education, Oxford, Basil Blackwell/The Open University.

BOOTH, T. (1987) 'Labels and their consequences', in LANE, D. and STRATFORD, B. (eds) *Current Approaches to Down's Syndrome*, London, Cassell.

BOOTH, T. (1988) 'Challenging conceptions of integration', in BARTON, L. (ed.) *The Politics of Special Educational Needs*, London, Falmer Press.

BOOTH, T. (1991) 'Integration, disability and commitment: A response to Marten Soder', *European Journal of Special Needs Education*, **6**, 1, pp. 1–15.

BOOTH, T. (1992) 'Reading Critically, Unit 10, "Learning for All"', Milton Keynes, The Open University.

BOOTH, T., SWANN, W. and POTTS, P. (eds) (1982) 'The Nature of Special Education the Practice of Special Education Course E241, "Special Needs in Education"', London, Croom Helm/The Open University Press.

BRENNAN, W. (1974) *Shaping the Education of Slow Learners*, London, Routledge and Kegan Paul.

BROUILLETTE, R. (1993a) 'Theories to explain the development of special education', in MITTLER, P., BROUILLETTE, R. and HARRIS, D. (eds) *Special Needs Education*, London, Kogan Page.

BROUILLETTE, R. (1993b) 'The future of special education: Who will pay the bill?' in MITTLER, P., BROUILLETTE, R. and HARRIS, D. (eds) *Special Needs Education 1993*, London, Kogan Page.

BURT, C. (1925) *The Young Delinquent*, London, University of London Press.

BURT, C. (1937) *The Backward Child*, London, University of London Press.

BURT, C. (1952) *The Causes and Treatment of Backwardness*, London, University of London Press.

BYERS, R. (1994) 'Teaching a dialogue: Teaching approaches and learning styles in schools for pupils with learning difficulties', in COUPE O'KANE, J. and SMITH, B. (eds) *Taking Control: Enabling People with Learning Difficulties*, London, David Fulton.

CAMPBELL, P. (1992) 'Introduction to Survivors' Poetry Anthology', *From Dark to Light*, London, Survivors' Press.

CASLING, P. (1993) 'Cobblers and song-birds: The language and imagery of disability', *Disability, Handicap and Society*, **8**, 2, pp. 203–10.

CHAPPELL, A.L. (1992) 'Towards a sociological critique of the normalisation principle', *Disability, Handicap and Society*, **7**, 1, pp. 35–52.

CLAIRE, H., MAYBIN, J. and SWANN, J. (eds) (1993) *Equality Matters: Case Studies for the Primary School*, Clevedon, Multilingual Matters Ltd.

CLARK, A. (1994) *Diaries*, London, Phoenix.

COOPER, C. (1996) 'Can a fat woman call herself disabled?', *Disability and Society*, forthcoming.

CORBETT, J. (1992) 'Careful teaching: Researching a special career', *British Educational Research Journal*, **18**, 3, pp. 235–44.

CORBETT, J. (1993) 'Postmodernism and the "special needs" metaphors', *Oxford Review of Education*, **19**, 4, pp. 547–54.

CORBETT, J. (1994a) 'Special language and political correctness', *British Journal of Special Education*, **21**, 1, pp. 17–19.

CORBETT, J. (1994b) 'A proud label: Exploring the relationship between disability politics and gay pride, *Disability and Society*, **9**, 3, pp. 343–57.

CORBETT, J. (1995) 'Rising Above It', *Survivors' Poetry Illustrated Anthology: Under The Asylum Tree*, London, Survivors' Press.

CORBETT, J. (1996) 'Teaching Special Needs: Tell me Where it Hurts?' Paper presented at American Educational Research Association 1996 Annual Conference, New York, April 8–12.

CORBETT, J. and RALPH, S. (1994) 'Empowering adults: The changing imagery of charity advertising', *Australian Disability Review*, **1**, 94, pp. 5–13.

CORTAZZI, M. (1993) *Narrative Analysis*, London, Falmer Press.

CRAFT, A. (ed.) (1994) *Practice Issues in Sexuality and Learning Disabilities*, London, Routledge.

CROSS, M. (1994) 'Abuse', in KEITH, L. (ed.) *Mustn't Grumble*, London, The Women's Press.

DES (1978) *Special Educational Needs: Report of the Committee of Enquiry into the Education of Handicapped Children and Young People*, London, HMSO.

DEVEREUX, K. (1982) *Understanding Learning Difficulties*, Milton Keynes, Open University Press.

DICKENSON, J. (1983) 'Some thoughts on fat', in SCHOENFIELDER, L. and WIESER, B. (eds) *Shadow on a Tightrope: Writings by Women on Fat Oppression*, Glasgow, Rotunda Press.

EARL, C.J.C. (1961) *Subnormal Personalities: Their Clinical Investigation and Assessment*, London, Bailliere, Tindall and Cox.

ELLISON, M. (1994) '"Disgusted" Bars Comic Eddy', *The Guardian*, 5th September 1994, p. 1.

ENGELBERG, E. (1989) *Elegiac Fictions: The Motif of the Unlived Life*, University Park, USA, Pennsylvania State University Press.

FAY, E.A. (ed.) (1893) *Histories of American Schools for the Deaf, 1817–1893*, Washington DC, The Volta Bureau.

FINKELSTEIN, V. (1980) *Attitudes and Disability Issues for Discussions*, New York, World Rehabilitation Fund.

FINKELSTEIN, V. (1993) 'The commonality of disability', in SWAIN, J., FINKELSTEIN, V., FRENCH, S. and OLIVER, M. (eds) *Disabling Barriers — Enabling Environments*, London, Sage and Open University and Press.

FITTON, P. (1994) *Listen To Me: Communicating the Needs of People with Profound Intellectual and Multiple Disabilities*, London, Jessica Kingsley.

FONTANA, D. (1994) *Managing Classroom Behaviour*, Leicester, British Psychological Society.

FOUCAULT, M. (1977) 'Power/knowledge: Selected Interviews and other writings, 1972–1977', edited by GORDON, C. in RABINOW, P. (ed.) *The Foucault Reader*, New York, Pantheon Books.

FRENCH, S. (1992) 'Simulation exercises in disability awareness training: A critique', *Disability, Handicap and Society*, **7**, 3, pp. 257–66.

FULCHER, G. (1989) *Disabling Policies?* London, Falmer Press.

GALLOWAY, D., ARMSTRONG, D. and TOMLINSON, S. (1994) *The Assessment of Special Educational Needs: Whose Problem?* London, Longman.

GERBER, D.A. (1990) 'Listening to disabled people: The problem of voice and authority', in ROBERT B. EDGERTON's 'The cloak of competence', *Disability, Handicap and Society*, **5**, 1, pp. 3–23.

GLAD (1995) *London Disability News*, London, Greater London Association of Disabled People.

GOFFMAN, E. (1961) *Asylums*, Harmondsworth, Penguin.

GOFFMAN, E. (1968) *Stigma: Notes on the Management of Spoiled Identity*, Harmondsworth, Penguin.

GORDON, J.C. (1892) *Notes and Observations upon the Education of the Deaf*, Washington D.C., The Volta Bureau.

GORDON, W. (1902) *Recollections of the Old Quarter*, Lynchburg, Virginia, Moose Bros. Company.

HETHERINGTON, R. (1974) 'The clinical interview', in MITTLER, P. (ed.) *The Psychological Assessment of Mental and Physical Handicaps*, London, Tavistock Publication & Methuen.

HEVEY, D. (1992) *The Creatures Time Forgot: Photography and Disability Imagery*, London, Routledge.

HOLMWOOD, C. (1994) 'Are we ready for a dramatic change?', *Asylum*, Summer 1994, **8**, 2, pp. 21–5.

HOYLE, E. and JOHN, P. (1995) *Professional Knowledge and Professional Practice*, London, Cassell.

INMAN, J. (1989) '"Bad" boys make good at Chelfham Mill', in WILDLAKE, P. (ed.) *Special Children Handbook*, London, Hutchinson.

JONES, K. (1992) 'Recognising successes and difficulties in learning', in JONES, K. and CHARLTON, T. *Learning Difficulties in Primary Classrooms*, London, Routledge.

KELMAN, J. (1994) *How Late It Was, How Late*, London, Quality Paperbacks Direct.

KIERNAN, C., JORDAN, R. and SAUNDERS, C. (1978) *Starting Off: Establishing Play and Communication in the Handicapped Child*, London, Souvenir Press.

LANE, H. (1984) *When the Mind Hears: A History of the Deaf*, New York, Random House.

LANE, J. (ed.) (1887) *Herbert Fry's Royal Guide to the London Charities*, London, Chatto and Windus.

LAWSON, M. (1995) 'Fugitives from the book police', *The Independent*, Tuesday, 31 January, p. 15.

LONGMORE, P. (1987) 'Elizabeth Bouvia, assisted suicide and social prejudice', *Issues in Law, and Medicine*, **3**, 2 (no page no given).

LOWSON, D. (1994) 'Understanding professional thought disorder: A guide for service users and a challenge for professionals', *Asylum*, Summer, **8**, 2, pp. 29–30.

MANNING, P. (1992) *Erving Goffman and Modern Sociology*, Stanford California, Stanford University Press.

MARCUS, E. (1992) *Making History: The Struggle for Gay and Lesbian Equal Rights 1945–1990*, New York, Harper Collins.

MITTLER, P. (ed.) (1974) *The Psychological Assessment of Mental and Physical Handicaps*, London, Methuen.

MORRIS, J. (1991) *Pride Against Prejudice*, London, The Women's Press.

MORRIS, J. (1992) 'Personal and political: A feminist perspective on researching physical disability', *Disability Handicap and Society*, **7**, 2, pp. 157–66.

MORRIS, J. (1994) 'The fall', in KEITH, L. (ed.) *Mustn't Grumble*, London, Women's Press.

MUIR, K. (1992) 'School is out, out, out', *Observer*, Sunday 26 July, p. 48.

McDONALD, P. (1994) 'Eurocentrism, ethnocentrism and social concepts', in BEGUM, N., HILL, M. and STEVENS, A. (eds) *Reflections: The Views of Black Disabled People on their Lives and Community Care*, London, Central Council for Education and Training in Social Work.

NG, P. (1992) 'The mental health rack', in *Survivors' Poetry Anthology, From Dark to Light*, London, Survivors' Press.

OLIVER, M. (1990) *The Politics of Disablement*, Basingstoke, Macmillan Education Ltd.

OLIVER, M. (1992a) 'Changing the social relations of research productions?', *Disability, Handicap and Society*, **7**, 2, pp. 101–14.

Oliver, M. (1992b) 'Intellectual masturbation: A rejoinder to Soder and Booth', *European Journal of Special Needs Education*, **7**, 1, pp. 20–8.

PAGLIA, C. (1992) *Sex, Art and American Culture*, London, Penguin Books.

PATTON, C. (1989) 'The AIDS industry: Construction of "victims", "volunteers" and "experts"', in CARTER, E. and WATNEY, S. (eds) *Taking Liberties: AIDS and Cultural Politics*, London, Serpent's Tail.

RENTERIA, D. (1993) 'Rejection', in LUCZAK, R. (ed.) *Eyes of Desire: A Deaf Gay and Lesbian Reader*, Boston, Alyson Publications.

RIESER, R. (1994) 'An opportunity not to be missed: 1994 inclusive school policies', *New Learning Together Magazine*, **1**, pp. 8–13.

RODENBURG, P. (1993) 'The Need for Words', London, Methuen Drama.

RUBIN SULEIMAN, S. (1994) *Risking Who One Is: Encounters with Contemporary Art and Literature*, Cambridge, Massachusetts, Harvard University Press.

SAMPSON LOW, J. (1850) *The Charities of London*, London, Sampson Low.

SANGER, J. (1995) 'Five easy pieces: The deconstruction of illuminatory data in research writing', *British Educational Research Journal*, **21**, 1, pp. 89–98.

SCHOENFIELDER, L. and WIESER, B. (eds) (1983) *Shadow on a Tightrope: Writings by Women on Fat Oppression*, Iowa, Aunt Lute Book Company.

SEDDON, T. (1994) *Context and Beyond: Reframing the Theory and Practice of Education*, London, Falmer Press.

SHAKESPEARE, T. (1993) 'Disabled people's self-organisation: A new social movement?' *Disability and Handicap Society*, **8**, 3, pp. 249–64.

SHAPIRO, J. (1993) *No Pity*, New York, Times Books.

SHOWALTER, E. (1991) *Sexual Anarchy: Gender and Culture at the Fin de Siecle*, London, Bloomsbury Publishing.

SILIN, J. (1993) 'New subjects, familiar roles: Progressive legacies in the postmodern world', in PIGNATELLI, F. and PFLAUM, S. (eds) *Celebrating Diverse Voices: Progressive Education and Equity*, Newbury Park, California, Corwin Press.

SILVERWOOD, A. (1994) 'Searching for disability arts', *Disability Arts Magazine (DAM)*, **413**, Autumn, pp. 2–5.

SODER, M. (1989) 'Disability as a social construct: The labelling approach revisited', *European Journal of Special Needs Education*, **4**, 2, pp. 117–29.

SODER, M. (1991) 'Theory, idealogy and research: A response to Tony

Booth', *European Journal of Special Needs Education*, **6**, 1, pp. 17–23.

SPENCE, J. (1986) *Putting Myself on the Picture*, London, Camden Press.

STEVENS, M. (1968) *Observing Children who are Severely Subnormal*, London, Edward Arnold.

STOTT, D., MARSTON, N. and NEILL, S. (1975) *Taxonomy of Behavior Disturbance*, London, University of London Press.

SZASZ, T. (1991) *The Untamed Tongue: A Dissenting Dictionary*, La Salle, Illinois, Open Court Publishing Co.

TAYLOR, A. (1991) *Prostitution: What's Love Got to Do With It?* London, MacDonald and Co. Ltd.

THEWELEIT, K. (1994) *Object — Choice*, London, Verso.

THOMPSON, B. (1994) *Sadomasochism: Painful Perversion or Pleasurable Play?* London Cassell.

TIZARD, J. (1966) 'Schooling for the handicapped', *Special Education: Incorporating Spastics' Quarterly*, Lv, 2, pp. 4–7.

TOMLINSON, S. (1981) *Educational Subnormality: A Study in Decision-Making*, London, Routledge and Kegan Paul.

TOMLINSON, S. (1982) *A Sociology of Special Education*, London, Routledge.

TORTON BECK, E. (ed.) (1989) *Nice Jewish Girls: A Lesbian Anthology*, Boston, Beacon Press.

WAITE, D. (1995) *Rethinking Instructional Supervision: Notes on its Language and Culture*, London, Falmer Press.

WALFORD, G. (1994) *Choice and Equity in Education*, London, Cassell.

WALFORD, G. (ed.) (1994) *Researching the Powerful in Education*, London, University College London Press.

WALTERS, K. (1994) *Re-Thinking Reason: New Perspectives in Critical Thinking*, Albany, State University of New York Press.

WALTER, N. (1994) 'Fundamentals of fundamentalism', *The Raven Anarchist Quarterly*, **7**, 3, pp. 221–36.

WARD, D. (1994) 'Brain damage boy caught in education tussle', *The Guardian*, September 12 1994, p. 4.

WHITTAKER, J. (1994) 'The myth of partnership', *New Learning Together Magazine*, **1**, April, pp. 22–29.

WILLIAMS, X. (1995) 'Some disabilities are more equal than others', *The Disability Rag*, May/April, pp. 6–9.

WINTERSON, J. (1994) *Art and Lies*, London, Jonathan Cape.

WHELAN, E., SPEAKE, B. and STRICKLAND, T. (1984) 'The Copewell Curriculum: Development, content and use', in DEAN, A. and HEGARTY, S. (eds) *Learning for Independence*, London, Further Education Unit.

WOLFENDALE, S. (ed.) (1993) *Assessing Special Educational Needs*, London, Cassell.

WRIGHT, H. (1966) 'Contribution of the school psychological service to special education', in *What is Special Education? The Proceedings of the First International Conference of the Association for Special Education*, Stanmore, Association for Special Education Ltd.

YULE, W. (1975) 'Psychological and medical concepts', in WEDELL, K. (ed.) *Orientations in Special Education*, London, John Wiley and Sons.

ZOLA, I.K. (1993) 'Self, identity and the naming question: Reflections on the language of disability', *Social Science and Medicine*, **36**, 2, pp. 167–73.

Index